3RD EDITION

SENIOR TEXT TYPES

A WRITING GUIDE FOR STUDENTS

ELLI **HOUSDEN**

Australia • Brazil • Mexico • Singapore • United Kingdom • United States

Senior Text Types: A Writing Guide for Students
3rd Edition
Elli Housden

Publishers: Alyssa Lanyon-Owen and Sam Bonwick
Project editor: Kathryn Coulehan
Editor: Nick Tapp
Proofreader: Julie Wicks
Cover designer: Petrina Griffin
Text designer: Belinda Davis
Cover image: iStockphoto/MG_54
Permissions researcher: Wendy Duncan
Production controller: Christine Fotis
Typeset by: Q2A Media

Acknowledgements
The publisher would like to credit and acknowledge the following sources for photographs: p. 3 Getty Images/iStock/g-stockstudio; p. 9 Shutterstock.com/Crdjan; p. 11 Getty Images/iStock/Pyrosky; p. 77 (left to right) Shutterstock.com/BlueOrange Studio, Alamy Stock Photo/Rrrainbow; p. 79 (top to bottom, left to right) Alamy Stock Photo/Blake Harrington III, Getty Images/iStock Unreleased/ampueroleonardo, Alamy Stock Photo/Anthony Lynn, Fairfax Syndication/Andrew Meares, imagefolk/Lopolo, Alamy Stock Photo/Hongqi Zhang, Alamy Stock Photo/JAY MID.

For product information and technology assistance,
in Australia call **1300 790 853**;
in New Zealand call **0800 449 725**

For permission to use material from this text or product, please email
aust.permissions@cengage.com

National Library of Australia Cataloguing-in-Publication Data
A catalogue record for this book is available from the National Library of Australia

Cengage Learning Australia
Level 7, 80 Dorcas Street
South Melbourne, Victoria Australia 3205

Cengage Learning New Zealand
Unit 4B Rosedale Office Park
331 Rosedale Road, Albany, North Shore 0632, NZ

For learning solutions, visit **cengage.com.au**

Printed in China by 1010 Printing International Limited.
7 8 9 10 25 24

Introduction

In this revised edition of *Senior Text Types: A Writing Guide for Students*, 39 text types or genres have been analysed. Each type of writing has been defined and explained according to its purpose and its generic features: structure and organisation, language and grammar. An annotated example of each text type has been provided as a model for students. In order to reflect real world presentation, where appropriate, text type examples are now presented in full colour. To complement these examples, there is a list of writing activities at the back of the book. Terms that appear in bold blue type are defined in the glossary.

This comprehensive guide will assist students to analyse and write coherently and accurately across a variety of genres.

Elli Housden

Contents

1 Definition

An advertisement is a text which sells a product or a service.

2 Purpose and role of writer

To promote, to persuade someone to buy a product or service

3 Generic features

Structure and organisation

- eye-catching layout that 'jumps off the page'
- simple and **uncluttered** text for clarity
- a mixture of written and visual text; bold and balanced
- focus on originality and readability; large bold print
- interesting font, contemporary and fashionable illustration

Language

- clear, accurate description to facilitate easy purchase
- persuasive or emotive language/**superlatives**, e.g. *must-have jeans*
- text must suit product, e.g. *blues*; *The faded blue*
- text must suit audience/potential buyer's tastes and needs, e.g. *the trendy you*
- use of statistics/humour/**testimonials**/rhyme/**alliteration**/exaggeration/repetition of keywords to **reinforce** an image, e.g. *blue*; *you*

Grammar

- **imperatives**, e.g. *Buy now!*
- **rhetorical questions**/**sentence fragments**, e.g. *Why are blues for you?*
- use of second person pronoun 'you', and the inclusive 'we'
- adjectives and verbs, e.g. *trendy*; *must-have*
- present tense, e.g. *Why are blues for you?*

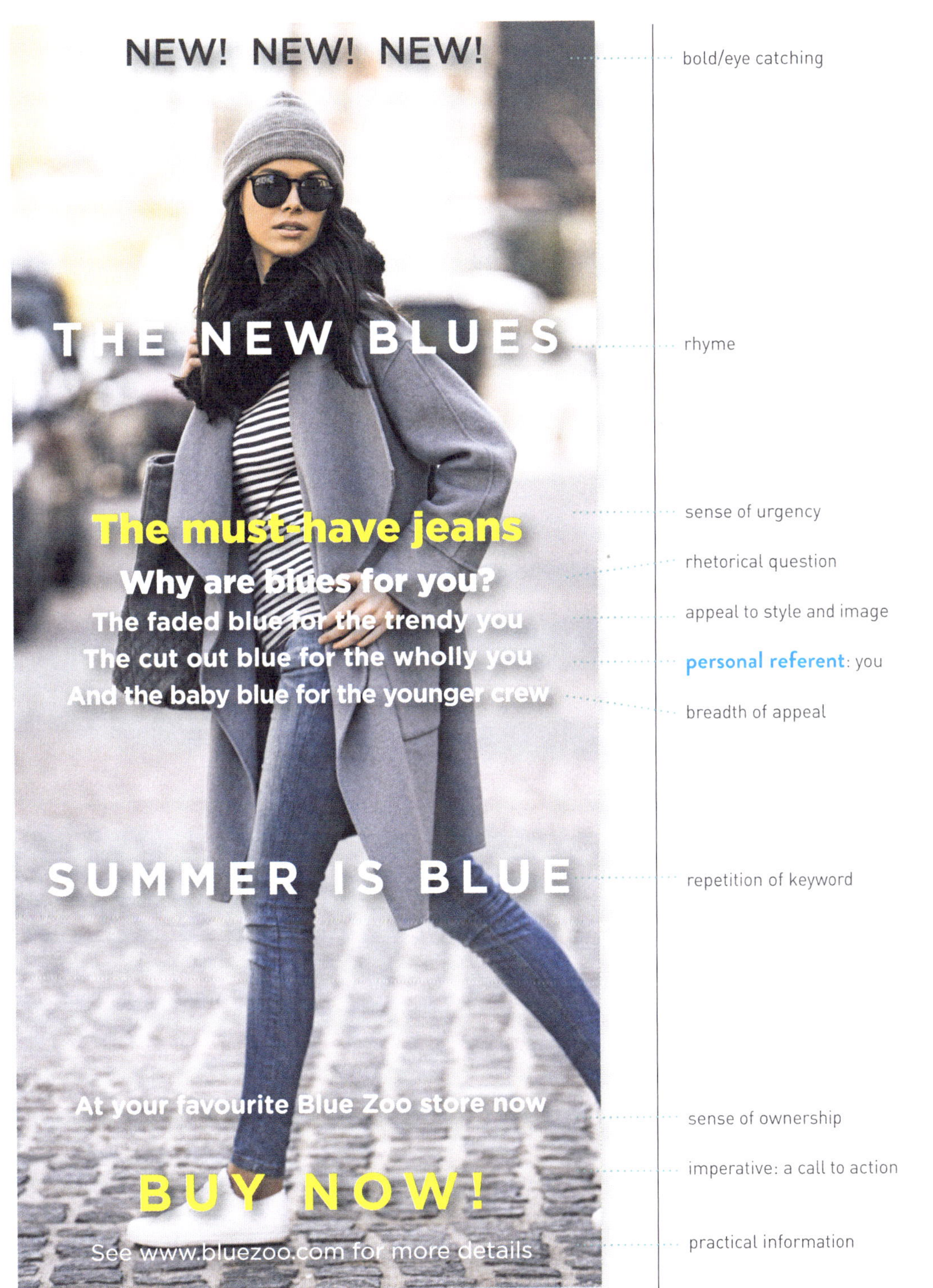
NEW! NEW! NEW!
THE NEW BLUES
The must-have jeans
Why are blues for you?
The faded blue for the trendy you
The cut out blue for the wholly you
And the baby blue for the younger crew
SUMMER IS BLUE
At your favourite Blue Zoo store now
BUY NOW!
See www.bluezoo.com for more details
bold/eye catching
rhyme
sense of urgency
rhetorical question
appeal to style and image
personal referent: you
breadth of appeal
repetition of keyword
sense of ownership
imperative: a call to action
practical information

1 Definition

An agenda is a program of business to be undertaken at a meeting. It is presided over by a chairperson.

Minutes are the written notes taken at a meeting by the secretary. These record what was discussed at the meeting for future reference and serve as a historical and legal record of the proceedings. Minutes are a nonfiction text.

2 Purpose and role of writer

To record information precisely and accurately; usually written by the secretary of the organisation

3 Generic features

Structure and organisation

- prescribed **format** and headings, e.g. *Agenda*; *Minutes*
- numeration in a list format

Language

- specific language associated with meetings, e.g. *Chair*; *Business arising*; *Other business*; *Minutes*
- clear, concise, factual language
- accurate transcription of spoken language
- may include quotes from participants

Grammar

- sentences and paragraphs
- sentence fragments, e.g. *moved*
- past tense, e.g. *opened*; *reported*; future tense, e.g. *Joe Crowley will ...*
- third person/impersonal, e.g. *he*, *they*

Agenda of the North West Football Club Committee Meeting 1 October 2017

1 **Minutes of the last meeting**

2 **Business arising**

3 **Reports:**
- Treasurer
- Director of Coaching

4 **Other business**

Prescribed format and **terminology**

Minutes of the North West Football Club Committee Meeting held at the North West Football Clubhouse on 1 October 2017

The meeting opened at 7 pm.

Chair: Matthew Jones

Prescribed format and terminology

Present: Jim Anderson, Nathan Bell, Liam Connors, Andrew Dent and Eddie Edwards

Accuracy

Apologies: Sandy Simpson, Joe Crowley

Minutes of the previous meeting: moved J. Anderson, seconded N. Bell, that the minutes of the September meeting be accepted as a true and accurate record.

Business arising from the minutes:

- Jim Anderson is to organise transport to next month's game at the Gold Coast.
- Eddie Edwards is to assist the Secretary for the rest of the year.

Concise factual language

Treasurer's report: moved L. Connors, seconded A. Dent, that the financial report be accepted.

Director of Coaching report: reported on injuries so far this season and fitness strategies for the rest of the season. Moved E. Edwards, seconded N. Bell that the coaching report be accepted.

Language is businesslike but formal

Other business:

- Sandy Simpson has agreed to organise the Christmas party.
- Joe Crowley will purchase the new footballs for next season.

Future tense

The chairperson closed the meeting at 9.10 pm.

Past tense

Next meeting: 3 November 2017

Conclusion

1 Definition

A biography is the story of a person's life told by another person.

2 Purpose and role of writer

To inform or reveal details of a person's life for historical or personal reasons, or for profit

3 Generic features

Structure and organisation

- book format; divided into chapters
- arrangement may be **chronological** or thematic, e.g. early years, schooldays, adult achievements
- content outlines noteworthy events from a person's life e.g. rites of passage, e.g. *When he was named Australian of the Year in 2014 ...*

Language

- usually formal, creating distance between writer and reader, e.g. *Recently, the Australian Rules code has become a platform for racial inclusiveness and equality.*
- generally factual and objective, depending on the writer's purpose
- language suits the historical and social **context**, e.g. *In 2013, he endured a racist slur from a young Collingwood supporter during a game at the MCG.*
- writer may influence the reader via **subjective** language or inclusion or omission of facts, e.g. *An apology was too little, too late ...*
- writing style should engage the reader through description to bring the subject to life

Grammar

- correct English in complete sentences
- third person used, perhaps with quotes from the person profiled
- past tense is more common because of content, e.g. *the AFL agreed that it had not done enough to protect Goodes from crowd abuse.*

Adam Goodes is not only a sporting hero; he is a role model for young footballers, especially those of Aboriginal origin. When he was named Australian of the Year in 2014, it was not so much for his brilliance on the AFL field as for his commitment to work in the community promoting Indigenous issues and speaking out against racism.

Formal, impersonal style/ opinionative in parts

Yet Goodes' career has not been without controversy. In 2013, he endured a racist slur from a young Collingwood supporter during a game at the MCG. This led, not to reconciliation, but to further racial tension in matches that followed. After being named as Australian of the Year, Goodes launched a campaign entitled 'Racism: it stops with me', standing up for himself in the media. Unfortunately, it didn't stop, and in hindsight, the AFL agreed that it had not done enough to protect Goodes from crowd abuse. An apology was too little, too late, and led to Goodes walking away from the game he loved and excelled at.

Use of past tense/specific references to dates and places

Goodes' departure from the game in 2016 was marred by ill feeling, the culmination of months of booing and abuse from the crowd. Hardly a fitting tribute for a player who held the record for the number of games played by an Indigenous footballer, a Brownlow medal winner – in short, an elite sportsman. Perhaps Goodes can take some solace from recent television campaigns to recruit young people from all racial origins into AFL. Recently, the Australian Rules code has become a platform for racial inclusiveness and equality.

Complex sentences/formal language

Goodes, too, since leaving the sporting field, has devoted his time to advancing the cause of Indigenous youth. Even before he was named Australian of the Year, Goodes with fellow Sydney Swans player, Michael O'Loughlin, had formed the Go Foundation, which provides scholarships to Indigenous youth in the inner suburbs of Sydney, so that they can be educated and be able to give back to their communities. Goodes recognises that education is vital in empowering youth to develop the skills and confidence to achieve their potential. Despite everything he has endured, Goodes is keen to give back to the community that encouraged his illustrious career.

Indirect quotes/personal referents

Not only is the Go Foundation expanding and gaining corporate support, but the message about racism will be highlighted in the art world this year. A portrait of Adam Goodes entitled 'Colour Doesn't Matter' by Megan Adams, a Darwin artist, has been entered in this year's Archibald Prize.

1 Definition

A post on a web page for a public audience, usually updated regularly

2 Purpose and role of writer

- To exchange information and opinions
- To promote a blogger's public profile
- To make new friends or followers through interactive communication
- To persuade readers to a point of view or the purchase of a product or brand

3 Generic features

Structure and organisation

- a title related to the purpose of the blog, e.g. *Cheers to my new 'poison'!*
- a photo of the author or a themed photo/s relating to the blog
- no set structure or organisation
- individual style and content, e.g. *Yep, I'm hitting the pavement ...*

Language

- may be formal and educational
- usually conversational and personal, e.g. *Anyway, I'm into the second week ...*
- **colloquialisms** and language appropriate to the chosen topic

Grammar

- first person, e.g. *I'm in training.*
- second person addresses the reader, e.g. *Did you know ...*
- short sentences, fragments, e.g. *And chilly too.*

Cheers to my new 'poison'!

I'm in training. Yep, I'm hitting the pavement at six am every morning in my new designer cross-trainers. Did you know it's still dark at that time in the morning? And chilly too. So, I'm loving my new Lorna Jane zip up jacket with matching hoodie.

Informal language/personal referents

Anyway, I'm into the second week, with the half-marathon on my mind. Only three months to go. Can I keep it up? I hope so. I've invested a few hundred dollars in the gear, especially the hot pink trainers. But it's all going to be worth it, I know it is.

Just wondering? What's your favourite poison? I don't mean alcohol or Coca Cola. I've given those up, of course. I was just wondering what other elite athletes (joke) fuel up with after the journey. Pure spring water or a yummy sports drink. What's your favourite colour? Flavour? What's your poison?

Conversational tone/use of rhetorical questions to include reader

Use of second person to include reader

If I run for half an hour, I can lose a whole litre of water from my body. How am I going to replace it? Should I drink water or what?

Use of first person

So, I've been doing some research …

Sports drinks contain water for hydration, salt to replace the sweat (called electrolytes – remember those fascinating chemistry lessons you thought were irrelevant) and sugar for re-boosting your energy levels. Sounds simple and harmless enough, hey, and tastes way better than water. Prettier colours too, if you want to co-ordinate them with your outfit.

Mix of factual and personal style

However, my friends, sports drinks are also acidic. Some brands contain more sugar than others. They can wreck your porcelain, pearly white smile and make a visit to the dentist an excruciating experience, if you overdose on them, as I've been doing until recently.

Water is better, some experts say. There is still debate in society as to how much water we should consume in an average day, whether we are exercising or not. Drink before you're thirsty or drink because you're thirsty. The jury's out. There's also some evidence that too much water can cause dangerously low levels of salt in the body, especially in athletes who top up constantly during marathons. This is thought to be dangerous, too.

Sales of both bottled water and sports drinks have skyrocketed in the last decade. Just the sports drink market is estimated to be worth over a billion dollars in Australia this year, while sales of bottled water have topped the two-billion-dollar mark.

Use of statistics to reinforce point of view

Gotta go! I'm heading out the door, armed with my lightly sparkling fizzy water.

Yes! Cheers, till next time!

1 Definition

A brochure is a small booklet or folded piece of A4 paper, designed for informational and promotional purposes.

A flyer is a single-page handbill or advertisement.

2 Purpose and role of writer

To inform and persuade; to 'sell' an idea or a service

3 Generic features

Structure and organisation

- divided into small logical sections according to subject and purpose
- information organised into smaller subtexts for easier interpretation
- eye-catching layout
- front cover should make purpose **explicit**
- inside pages should contain more detailed text
- some use of visual text, e.g. maps/illustrations
- attractive illustration; variety of fonts to create visual appeal

Language

- clear and concise language, e.g. *Open all day till 10 pm*
- informative/persuasive language, e.g. *Gourmet menu*; *Takeaway available*
- language must suit product or service, e.g. *a place to relax*
- factual and persuasive words, e.g. *fragrant aroma*
- language must appeal to target group, e.g. *haven from the outside world*

Grammar

- short sentences/fragments/imperatives, e.g. *Come to*
- rhetorical questions, e.g. *Looking for a haven from the outside world?*
- present tense, e.g. *Imagine*
- use of the second person pronoun 'you' or the inclusive 'we'

* OPENING SOON *

Imagine the fragrant aroma of freshly roasted beans mingled with newly baked bread — Adjectives and verbs appeal to the senses

Looking for a haven from the outside world? — Emotive word (*haven*)

Come to **Cafe Bellissima** –
a place to relax with friends — Appeal to social factors

Hope to see you soon. — Use of inclusive 'you'

• Gourmet menu • Courtyard setting • Takeaway available — Message is clear and concise

Cafe Bellissima

75 Cappuccino Street Coffeetown
Ph: 3380 7166 — Practical information

Open for breakfast from 7 am

Open all day till 10 pm

1 Definition

A description is an illustration of a topic or object in words.

2 Purpose and role of writer

To explain or to make the reader see the text

3 Generic features

Structure and organisation

- Descriptions are written in paragraphs, divided into sentences
- Informative descriptions
  - use of topic sentences as **signposts** for the reader
  - are logical in development, e.g. *Fish Lane is one of the oldest streets in the city.*
- **Literary** descriptions
  - are usually the part of a text that also contains action, dialogue and reflection, e.g. *There's hungry dogs that salivate and bare their teeth if you fight them for the scraps.*
  - may be less structured

Language

- Informative descriptions
  - use concrete and precise factual language, e.g. *Before 1904, it was known as Soda Water Lane ...*
  - generally objective and unbiased
  - generally formal and impersonal, e.g. *Located on the corner of Melbourne Street is the Fox Hotel ...*
- Literary descriptions
  - use literal as well as **metaphorical** language
  - use **imagery** and the language of the senses, e.g. *hissing and growling like dogs*
  - use strong verbs and adjectives
  - create mood through language choices, e.g. *the rag-tag mob that slink in the shadows after dark*
  - may be personal, subjective and informal

Grammar

- Informative descriptions
  - present or past tense
  - usually in third person, e.g. *Today, it is a hub of restaurants ...*
  - mixture of sentence types, e.g. *Situated in West End ...*
- Literary descriptions
  - may be first, second or third person
  - choice of tense
  - may use sentence fragments, e.g. *Not that they're all friendly.*

Informative description

Fish Lane is one of the oldest streets in the city.

Situated in West End, it is named after Mr Fish, who was a local alderman.

Before 1904, it was known as Soda Water Lane, though no one knows why. Today, it is a hub of restaurants and bars. Seafood features as one choice but there is also a pizzeria and a couple of bars serving snacks, but specialising in boutique beer and wine. There are also cafes serving an array of blends, both traditional and exotic. Located on the corner of Melbourne Street is the Fox Hotel, famous since Expo 88 put South Brisbane and West End firmly on the tourist and gourmet map.

The proximity of Fish Lane to the Cultural Centre precinct, with its Performing Arts Complex on one side of Melbourne Street and the Gallery of Modern Art (GOMA), Museum and State Library on the other, makes it an ideal place to dine before or after cultural events. Yet, Fish Lane is just one street in this inner-city locale. Turning southwards from the lane will take the visitor to the centre of West End, with its Asian and European restaurants, cafes and bars. Turn northward and it is a short walk across the Victoria Bridge into the CBD.

Topic sentence signposts content of paragraph

Information is objective and unbiased

Use of present tense and formal language in an objective style

Literary description

Fish Lane is one of the oldest streets in the city. Its best feature is the cafes that line one side of the narrow lane, each offering different smells – and tastes too, if you are quick enough. And it's not just fish.

No wonder that the homeless, the dregs of society, huddle together in Fish Lane. Tom wouldn't have survived without learning from the others, the rag-tag mob that slink in the shadows after dark. Not that they're all friendly. There's hungry dogs that salivate and bare their teeth if you fight them for the scraps. Even worse are the feral cats that emerge in the early hours of the morning, sometimes in packs, hissing and growling like dogs. Some are bigger than the dogs and more ferocious. Tom is glad that he's small enough to squeeze behind the row of bins opposite the fish and chip shop.

Fish Lane wasn't named for its seafood, though Tom doesn't know that. All Tom knows is the struggle to stay alive. And people are an even bigger threat than the wild creatures that stalk the city at night. Even for a tomcat.

Use of second person 'you' to gain the reader's attention

Imagery creates mood and visual effects

Street is seen through the eyes of a fictional character for dramatic purposes

1 Definition

An editorial is the expression of the viewpoint of the newspaper on an issue, written by the editor or an experienced senior journalist.

2 Purpose and role of writer

Opinionative writing designed to persuade the reader to a point of view and, sometimes, to take action on a selected issue

3 Generic features

Structure and organisation

- introduction: presents **hypothesis** or point of view, e.g. *especially those already suffering from the effects of a gambling addiction?*
- some background information on the issue may be given
- each paragraph:
  - must support the basic argument presented in the introduction
  - must have a clear topic sentence and then elaborate on the issue, giving one reason or example per paragraph; a logical and sequential development, e.g. *Australia is a nation of gamblers.*
- opinion must be supported with factual evidence, e.g. *Total gambling ... exceeds $1000.*
- conclusion: sometimes a strong statement, or a call for action to readers, e.g. *responsible government in line with majority public opinion*
- no **byline**

Language

- headline: short and sometimes clever; using humour or **irony** and an authoritative tone
- language: persuasive, sometimes emotive language used to hook readers, e.g. *replenish the coffers*; *mouths platitudes about 'responsible' gaming*
- formal educated language
- statistics used to support the arguments
- use of linking words

Grammar

- complex sentences mixed with shorter ones for emphasis
- longer paragraphs than in a news article
- rhetorical questions may be posed, e.g. *But what will it do ...?*
- third person point of view, though sometimes the inclusive 'we'/'our' or the **adversarial** 'they'/'them' is used, e.g. *Did you know that we spend ...?*
- present tense

Gambling pays off – but who wins?

Work began on the new Brisbane casino development early 2017 with some disruption to the flow of traffic.

Set to transform the face of the Queen's Wharf reach of the Brisbane River, the new casino development may enhance the tourist industry's profits and replenish the coffers of the state government. But what will it do for the people of the city, especially those already suffering from the effects of a gambling addiction?

Background information/negative **angle**

Doubtless, this unfortunate section of the population will increase as the opportunities to feed money into new 'one-armed bandits' are extended further.

Persuasive language/complex sentences

Australia is a nation of gamblers. Did you know that we spend more on gambling than any other nation in the world? Total gambling expenditure over a year per head of population exceeds $1000. Over three-quarters of this figure is spent on gaming. And this in a country where 75% of people think gambling should be more tightly controlled.

Use of statistics

Why? Because gambling can lead to addiction and addiction can lead to bankruptcy, marital and family breakup, depression and, in worst case scenarios, suicide. Gambling venues are associated with other addictions, such as smoking areas and alcohol sales. Some casinos offer free drinks to players at gambling tables. Then there is the perceived atmosphere of glamour and luxurious surroundings. All traps for even seasoned players.

Emotive language

Given the negative consequences of gambling and public concern about an industry that is expanding, why do governments not act more responsibly? Why has the Queensland Government welcomed the Queen's Wharf development? The answer is simple and predictable. Revenue! The state government, like its counterparts in other Australian states, mouths platitudes about 'responsible' gaming while accepting donations from the gambling lobby. Last year, the revenue raised by governments nationwide from the gambling industry exceeded five billion dollars. Is it any wonder that all stakeholders are rubbing their hands with glee?

Present tense/third person/critical tone

The new casino will be finished in 2022 and will replace the Treasury Casino in the city. This is small comfort to those who see the effects of a gambling addiction on a friend or a member of their family. No one is advocating a nanny state, only responsible government in line with majority public opinion.

Strong, authoritative conclusion

1 Definition

A comparative essay compares two similar or contrasting subjects. A comparative literary essay compares two texts.

2 Purpose and role of the writer

To inform and persuade the reader about the similarities and differences between two texts

3 Generic features

Structure and organisation

- introduction
  - a general comment that links two texts, e.g. *both concerned with issues of race*
  - provides background information
  - presents a clear point of view, e.g. *paint a negative picture of racial inequality.*
- body of the essay
  - devotes equal space to both texts
  - outlines the comparative and contrasting features of two texts
  - each paragraph is signposted with a topic sentence, e.g. *Scout Finch is shocked ...*
  - each paragraph provides evidence and examples from the text
- conclusion restates general points, e.g. *Both authors have written provocative texts ...*

Language

- formal, informative, persuasive
- comparative words, e.g. *both*, *also*, *echo*
- linking words, e.g. *Writing in the same era*; *however*
- metalanguage, e.g. *classic*, *set*, *coming of age novel*

Grammar

- variety of sentence type and length, generally complex
- present tense
- third person impersonal generally preferred over first person

Example

The classic American novel, *To Kill a Mockingbird* (1965) by Harper Lee, and the poems of the late Indigenous Australian writer, Oodgeroo Noonuccal, are both concerned with issues of race, and paint a negative picture of racial inequality.

Both texts mentioned

Set in the American South, *To Kill a Mockingbird* is a coming of age novel, narrated by Scout, the ten-year-old daughter of the town lawyer, Atticus Finch. Scout's father has brought his children up to treat all people, regardless of age and race, as equals. Their African-American housekeeper commands respect, and is a substitute mother figure for Scout and her brother, Jem. However, the Finch family are in the minority in their racial attitudes in the Deep South in the 1930s.

Background information

Writing in the same era as Harper Lee (1926–2016), racial issues also dominate the poetry of Oodgeroo Noonuccal (1920–1993). Born on Stradbroke Island and a member of the Noonuccal peoples, Oodgeroo has used her poetry to highlight the injustices of the Aboriginal people, to promote their advancement and to reform a system that has been discriminatory. Lee's novels echo these egalitarian sentiments, in defence of the African American people.

Background information

Scout Finch is shocked as events unfold in *To Kill a Mockingbird*. Through a child's eyes, we see what happens when a black American is accused of raping a white girl in Maycomb. When Atticus agrees to defend Tom Robinson, Scout becomes aware of the extent of racial hatred in the town, especially when she is a victim of it. Her father, a man of conscience, reassures her that 'real courage is when you know you're licked before you begin, but you begin anyway and see it through no matter what.'

Plot and character analysed

'Son of Mine' by Oodgeroo Noonuccal is also an attempt by a parent to educate a child about racism. The poet addresses her son, Denis, in a positive way, telling him 'of brave and fine' rather than 'brutal wrong and deeds malign'. Both authors are emphasising that no one can generalise about racism. Oodgeroo refers to 'rape and murder' and 'deeds malign', but the speaker in the poem, like Atticus Finch, prefers to emphasise times when 'black and white entwine'.

Content of poem analysed and compared to novel

Both authors have written provocative texts in an era of inequality. Both texts, *To Kill a Mockingbird* by Harper Lee and 'Son of Mine' by Oodgeroo Noonuccal, explore the negative aspects of racism and the positive aspects of acceptance of people, no matter what their colour or creed, which Oodgeroo refers to as a time when 'men in brotherhood combine'.

Conclusion restates general features in both texts

1 Definition

A persuasive essay presents a writer's point of view on an issue.

2 Purpose and role of writer

To persuade using appropriate information and writing style

3 Generic features

Structure and organisation

- expository structure, outlining and supporting a point of view
- introduction presents a hypothesis, e.g. *there has been great debate ...*
- body of the essay develops the argument step by step
- topic sentences summarise and signpost the argument, e.g. *Today, we have other options.*
- conclusion restates and clinches the argument

Language

- formal language, e.g. *It is ironic that Australia has more hours of available sunlight ...*
- key terms, related to the topic
- persuasive vocabulary, e.g. *There is no doubt ...*
- linking words to create cohesion

Grammar

- paragraph format
- complex sentences mixed with short statements for impact, e.g. *As the natural resources ... our pre-industrial forebears*
- present tense dominates
- inclusive pronouns, e.g. *we*; *our*

Let nature do the work!

In recent years, there has been great debate about climate change and global warming. A growing lobby of people are increasingly vocal about the adverse effect man is having on the planet. However, climate deniers see the latest changes as cyclical or non-existent.

Introduction makes the key general point

Whether climate change is caused by man or not, is academic. There is no doubt, that to preserve the health of the planet and its inhabitants, we need to address pollution caused by fossil fuels like coal, oil and gas. Not only do these substances damage the natural environment, but they are also unrenewable.

Topic sentence signposts paragraph

Uses appropriate language

It is now 200 years since the beginning of Industrial Revolution, when rural life in Britain was replaced by a mass movement of labour to industrial cities. In that era, coal was 'king', powering factories, transport and shipping. People were forced to live with the by-products of this age, notably air pollution, in cramped and overcrowded urban areas.

Sentences are lengthy and complex

Tone is serious to reflect content

Today, we have other options. As the natural resources of the planet are diminishing and will eventually be completely exhausted, we can turn the clock back to use the natural forms of energy discovered by our pre-industrial forebears. This is renewable energy that never runs out.

Present tense

Inclusive pronouns

Solar energy has been discussed and debated for nearly a century, but it is a relatively new form of power in comparison to that of water and wind. The Chinese claim to have used water mills for 2000 years and the ancient Greeks and Romans both constructed windmills to grind their grain. So, those who criticise renewable forms of energy as new and unreliable are mistaken.

Persuasive techniques

Informative content

In the new millennium, the main emphasis is on solar energy. It is ironic that Australia has more hours of available sunlight than most other nations, and yet we lag behind the rest of the world in its use and development. Short-sighted governments continue to talk up coal and natural gas, supporting these industries, despite the cost of production and their negative effects on the environment.

Complex sentences

The good news is that solar power in Australia is a growing industry that has increased fourfold in the last five years. However, solar still represents less than five per cent of the country's electricity output. Other nations have committed to phasing out fossil fuel in favour of renewables, and we need to follow suit. Given Australia's endorsement of the Kyoto Protocol and its support of the recent Climate Change Conference in Paris, it is hoped that eventually our future will be clean, green, cheap, renewable and everlasting.

Strong ending shows conviction

1 Definition

A feature article is an article written to give more depth to the news. Written by an expert, it gives background information on a newsworthy topic as well as the writer's personal slant or experience.

2 Purpose and role of writer

To inform and entertain, and sometimes to persuade

3 Generic features

Structure and organisation

- headline should be attention-grabbing, e.g. *Schoolies rules!*
- subheading, e.g. *Ask any school leaver. Schoolies Week has become a modern rite of passage.*
- byline, e.g. *Sebastian Penn*
- column format
- introduction should hook readers and establish a point of view through direct statement, example or rhetorical question, e.g. *Is that a rite or a right?*
- narrative rather than inverted pyramid structure

Language

- creative and colourful, e.g. *an extravagant pagan ritual*
- use of anecdotes or background information, e.g. *Melissa said*
- personal referents may be used
- **figurative language** may be used, e.g. *like an extravagant pagan ritual*
- writer creates relationship with reader through an individual writing style
- expansive, not economical, in length

Grammar

- use of first person is acceptable
- variety of long and short sentences
- present tense, e.g. *alcohol abuse is more common …*

Schoolies rules!

Catchy headline using assonance

Ask any school leaver. Schoolies Week has become a modern rite of passage. Sebastian Penn reports.

Subheading provides angle or point of view; byline

Is that a rite or a right? Certainly school leavers seem to believe that they deserve an all-out celebration at the end of 12 or 13 years of schooling. So don't expect this mega-indulgent festival to disappear in the near future.

Rhetorical question to hook readers and angle/point of view

Because it's become an institution, Schoolies Week has become more regimented and better controlled than in its early years. There is a large police presence, as well as council, community groups and volunteers who organise alcohol-free activities on the beach, day and night. And there have even been some positive spin-offs.

Complex sentence

Sentence fragment

When Schoolies Week began in the 1980s, there was little organisation or support for teenagers. This led a priest from the Oblate Order, Paul Costello, to found Rosies Youth Mission to support young people. Now Rosies has branched out into other areas, including support for the homeless.

Historical background supports point of view

There's also a website now that provides information on all aspects of Schoolies Week. Here schoolies are made aware of the consequences of underage drinking and the other pitfalls of post-school partying.

Informative content

One survey conducted after the celebration suggests that alcohol abuse is more common among males than females, with an average of 52.3% of males admitting to being drunk every day of the Schoolies Week. Figures relating to casual sexual partners and drug abuse are much more conservative.

Use of statistics

Yet, a number of girls interviewed after schoolies week spoke of being victims of sexual assault. Melissa (not her real name) said: 'I hooked up with Nathan and went back to his place. He forced himself on me, but he was pretty wasted, so I pushed him out of the way and ran home.' More in-school preventive programs are needed to educate students about the legal and safety issues that arise during schoolies week like consensual versus non-consensual sex, binge drinking, drink spiking and drug use.

Linking word

Anecdotal evidence

Opinionative content

So, even if Schoolies Week seems like an extravagant pagan ritual to parents and the older generation, every year it becomes more of a permanent fixture. And now that the term 'schoolies' has been legitimised by making its way into the *Oxford English Dictionary*, there is certainly no turning back.

Signposts a summing up

Conclusion links to introduction and angle of the article

1 Definition

A letter of application for a job is a letter that responds to a specific position.

2 Purpose and role of writer

To gain employment by impressing a prospective employer with relevant content and competent writing skills

3 Generic features

Structure and organisation

- sender's address is set out at the top on the left side of the page
- the date is placed underneath
- receiver's title and name, company name and address are set out below the date
- standard greeting, e.g. *Dear*
- the body of the letter is structured logically: introductory, explanatory and concluding paragraphs
- some use of persuasive language, e.g. *topped my year*; *good social skills*

Language

- formal (not impersonal) language, e.g. *as advertised in the* Local News
- terminology specific to business letters, e.g. *Yours faithfully*
- concise and clear
- positive, enthusiastic tone

Grammar

- formal grammar
- present tense, e.g. *I am also an outgoing person*
- first person, e.g. *I am writing to apply*

1 South Brisbane St
South Brisbane Qld 4101

Correct layout/format

1 December 2017
The Editor
The Local News
1 Brisbane St
Brisbane Qld 4000

Dear Sir/Madam

I am writing to apply for the position of cadet reporter as advertised in the *Local News* on Saturday 30 November.

Clear statement of purpose

I have just completed Year 12 at South Brisbane High School, where I topped my year in English, and was editor of the school newsletter. Next year I hope to enrol in a part-time degree in Journalism at the University of Queensland.

Background factual information

Not only do I love writing, but my teachers and the school's Careers Counsellor have advised me to pursue my talents in this area. I am also an outgoing person with good social skills and the ability to work in a team.

Personal qualities appropriate for the position

For two years I have worked as a waitress at the Bellissima Cafe in Queen Street, Brisbane. Here I have learnt communication skills and how to interact with the public. I know this experience will stand me in good stead in the newspaper industry.

Previous experience

Skills acquired

Link to new position

I look forward to hearing from you.

Yours faithfully

Standard closure

Ann Applicant

Ann Applicant

1 Definition

A resume is a record of personal details which is attached to the letter. A resume contains a written summary of educational qualifications, employment history and personal details. It is also called a curriculum vitae (CV).

2 Purpose and role of writer

To gain employment

3 Generic features

Structure and organisation

- arranged chronologically according to the definition above
- numerical structure with headings
- summary list format
- logical sequence
- attractively formatted
- designed for ease and speed of reading

Language

- concise but formal
- factual and accurate

Grammar

- sentence format
- sentence fragments
- third person
- past tense to describe past achievements

Resume

Name:	Ann Applicant	Correct layout and format
Address:	1 South Brisbane Street South Brisbane Qld 4101	Logically structured response
Telephone:	(07) 3844 4444	
Email:	annapplicant@hotmail.com	
Education:	South Brisbane Primary School (2007–13) South Brisbane State High School (2013–17) Completed Queensland Senior – 2017	Use of dates for clarity
Employment:	Cafe Bellissima: Queen Street, City (2013–17) Duties include: table service, barista, some food preparation. Pizza Palace: King Street, City (2012–13) Duties included: taking orders across the counter and by telephone, some food preparation, use of cash register. The City News: 1 Elizabeth Street, City (2011–12) Duties included: folding and adding inserts to newspapers, delivery of newspapers.	Clear description of tasks and skills
Personal qualifications:	Dux of English 2015, 2017 Debating Captain 2017 Editor of the school newsletter 2016, 2017 Student editor of the school annual 2016 Girl Guide Leader 2014, 2015 Member of Second IV Tennis 2014	Evidence of applicant's qualities
Referees:	Maria Bellissima, Cafe Proprietor – Ph: 3010 0000 Susan English, Teacher, South Brisbane State High School – Ph: 3010 1111	Contact details

1 Definition

A job interview is a meeting between an employer and a prospective employee.

2 Purpose and role of writer

The employer's purpose is to choose the most suitable applicant for the job through effective questioning. The prospective employee's role is to persuade the employer or interviewer that he or she is the most suitable person for the job.

3 Generic features

Structure and organisation

- Interviewer will determine the structure of the interview, e.g. *So you want to be a journalist?*
- She or he will provide some background information about the job and expectations, e.g. *Well, let me tell you ...*
- Interviewer is likely to refer to the applicant's written application/resume to develop a line of questioning, e.g. *And I see you're good at English.*
- Interviewer will probably cover the three aspects in the resume: education, previous employment and personal qualifications, by questioning the prospective employee in more detail, e.g. *And do you think your results will be good enough to get you into Journalism at university?*
- Interviewee must give the employer eye contact and respond clearly and concisely, with honesty, sincerity and interest. Be positive.
- At the end of, or during, the interview, the interviewee will be encouraged to ask questions about the job. These should be carefully thought out, and not merely concerned with pay and conditions, e.g. *How long do you think it will be before I publish a story?*

Language

- informal but deferential (showing respect)
- politeness, combined with an enthusiastic tone of voice, is essential
- good vocabulary, especially related to the terminology of the job, e.g. *editing the school newsletter*; *writing skills*; *Microsoft Office*

Grammar

- correct grammar
- spoken mode so sentence fragments are acceptable
- first person

Employer:	Good morning, Applicant. (indicating a seat)	
Applicant:	Good morning. (sits)	
Employer:	So you want to be a journalist?	
Applicant:	(looking at employer) Yes. I decided on my chosen career two years ago, after I began editing the school newsletter.	Relevant, definite answers/ concise responses
Employer:	And I see you're good at English.	
Applicant:	Yes, it's my favourite subject. It's helped with my writing skills.	
Employer:	And do you think your results will be good enough to get you into Journalism at university?	
Applicant:	I think so. I certainly hope so.	Honest, sincere response
Employer:	And what about your IT skills?	
Applicant:	I learnt to use Microsoft Office at school and I'm quite fast and accurate at word processing. I've also just started a blog.	
Employer:	Good. Well, let me tell you a little about the job. If you were the successful applicant, we would train you by sending you out with some of our senior journalists. They'll show you how to gather information and interview people. Then they'll show you how to write a story. We'd begin with small stories. You'd be required to do some office work and general errands, too. How does that sound?	
Applicant:	Great. How long do you think it would be before I published a story?	Positive attitude/enthusiasm
Employer:	Well, that would really depend on you and your expertise. Of course it's only a part-time position. We'd give you time off to attend your lectures.	
Applicant:	Thank you. And is there any likelihood that this position would become a full-time one when I graduate?	Questions show enthusiasm and competence
Employer:	Yes, there's every possibility that we'd keep you on after graduation if you proved satisfactory.	
Applicant:	That's great.	
Employer:	Your CV looks very good. We just have one or two more applicants to interview before we make a final decision. We'll let you know by Friday. Do you have any other questions?	
Applicant:	Just one. How can I prepare myself for the job? I read a lot of newspapers on the Internet and keep up with current affairs.	Question shows interest and confidence
Employer:	That's a great start. Keep reading and learning. And we'll let you know by the end of the week ...	

1 Definition

A business letter is a procedural form of communication. Any letter that is not personal (i.e. to family or friends) is considered a business letter.

2 Purpose and role of writer

To seek or impart information of a personal business or general business nature

3 Generic features

Structure and organisation

- sender's address set out on the left side of the page
- the date placed below the sender's address
- receiver's title and name, company name and address set out below the date, e.g. *The Manager, Sonyano Pty Ltd*
- the standard greeting, e.g. *Dear*; the closure, e.g. *Yours faithfully*
- logical structure in the body of the letter: introductory, explanatory and concluding paragraphs

Language

- impersonal language, e.g. *Then, for no apparent reason*; *Furthermore*
- business terminology, e.g. *a refund*; *the manufacturer*; *to compensate*
- concise and direct, e.g. *I have attached the sales docket*
- tone is polite and businesslike

Grammar

- formal grammar
- complex sentences
- first person, e.g. *I am writing to complain*
- present tense, e.g. *I am accumulating fines*

Example

1 Sydney Street
Sydney NSW 2000

1 February 2017

The Manager
Sonyanyo Pty Ltd
1 Company Road
North Sydney NSW 2060

Dear Sir/Madam

I am writing to complain about the Sonyano video game console, Model 356Z , that I purchased recently from a local electrical store. After I unpacked and assembled the machine, it worked perfectly for about a week. Then, for no apparent reason, when I pressed 'play', it refused to work. Furthermore, from that moment the 'open–close' device on the console refused to operate at all. To make matters worse, the optical disc that is stuck in the machine is borrowed from the local library, and it is now nine days overdue.

I have returned the console to the electrical store and they have given me a refund for the machine, which they assure me will be returned to you, the manufacturer. However, JC Electrical refuses to compensate me for the disc that is stuck in the machine, and for which I am accumulating fines owed to the library. The amount of these fines is growing daily, but I do not feel that it is my responsibility to pay this overdue fee.

I have attached the sales docket for the game console as proof of my purchase, and the borrowing slip for the disc from the library. Could you please call Mr Elton Presley at the library and arrange payment for the overdue disc? This situation, as you can see, has caused me some distress. I would appreciate it if you could advise me when this problem has been resolved.

Yours faithfully

John Payne

Standard layout and format

Clear statement of purpose/ clear statement of the problem

Concise outline of the problem presents a strong case and a legitimate complaint

Conclusion requests action politely and firmly

1 Definition

A letter to the editor is a business letter written to a newspaper. Most letters are now sent by email.

2 Purpose and role of writer

To express an opinion on an issue

3 Generic features

Structure and organisation

- use business letter format if sending by mail
- if emailing, use the greeting: *Sir/Madam* or *Dear Sir/Madam*
- introduction outlines the topic and the writer's opinion, e.g. *We live in a society …*
- body paragraphs develop the argument logically, point by point, including **rebuttal**
- topic sentences provide clear signposts, e.g. *The media clearly bears some of the blame*
- conclusion restates opinion, or is a call to action or solution, e.g. *They deserve better!*

Language

- formal/impersonal, e.g. *Personality has taken the place of policy*
- vocabulary appropriate to the issue raised
- informative but also forceful and persuasive, e.g. *Isn't it a shame*
- use of examples, e.g. *the leaders of major parties*
- use of statistics, e.g. *barely in double figures*
- dramatic, emotional or use of irony to provoke a response from readers, e.g. *resorting instead to venting and character assassination*
- topic sentences as signposts, e.g. *No wonder the young people of today*

Grammar

- complete and correct sentences and paragraphs
- present or past tense, e.g. *The media clearly bears some of the blame …*
- first person is acceptable, as are second and third person. Second person (you) or first person plural (we) may be used as a form of persuasion, e.g. *our political leaders*
- rhetorical questions are effective, e.g. *What sort of future is this for the young of today?*

Sir/Madam

We live in a society that has lost its way. And I believe that our political leaders are largely to blame. Personality has taken the place of policy, and the idea of a life devoted to public service is nowhere to be seen. Prominent figures from all sides of politics behave as though the public exists to serve them, rather than the reverse.

What sorts of values are being passed down to the next generation by the leaders of major parties? Isn't it a shame that such talent is so misdirected? And it's not only the leaders of the major parties who are guilty of behaving badly and presenting as poor role models to the younger generation. Ministers of government and members of both houses of parliament seem more concerned to shore up their own personal power and influence than to exert a good influence on the future of our country.

No wonder the young people of today are so disengaged from politics. Not only teenagers either. Young adults, who should be stepping forward to take responsibility and lead us into the future, are instead stepping away and rejecting the democratic process, resorting instead to venting and character assassination on social media.

The media clearly bears some of the blame for this outrage, and social media especially. The platforms that held out such hope for a better future, underpinned by technology, have become the playthings of anyone who seeks to manipulate opinion. What sort of future is this for the young of today? They deserve better!

A. Luddite
Marylands

Standard greeting

Clear opening, presenting clear point of view with examples

Use of rhetorical questions/ topic sentences to signpost argument/examples

Sentence fragments for impact/emotive language

Dramatic conclusion and final sentence

Today there is an abundance of choice for teens, even in the **genre** of teenage romance. The shelves of school and local libraries are packed with intriguing titles. The audience for these, as with their adult equivalent, is generally female.

1 Definition

Young adult fiction describes texts that are written and published for a teenage market.

2 Purpose and role of writer

To interest teenagers in reading and purchasing a product

3 Generic features

Structure and organisation

- narrative/story structure
- chapter format – often fast-moving, short chapters
- plot – usually dramatic and suspenseful, involving conflict between teenagers or adults
- characters – main protagonist is generally a teenage character
- setting – usually familiar: home, school, etc.
- narrative voice – action is seen through the eyes of a teenage hero or heroine

Language

- must be suitable to a teenage audience
- should replicate contemporary teen expressions, lifestyle and icons
- dialogue must be realistic according to character and situation
- description should be brief and visual so as not to interrupt the storyline
- style may be reflective if first person is used
- depending on audience age, swearing and some sexually explicit material is acceptable
- writing style must create atmosphere and strong emotion to maintain audience interest

Grammar

- written in first or third person
- may use multiple narration
- mixture of simple and complex sentences
- dialogue use may be ungrammatical, depending on characters' ages and level of education
- adjectives and adverbs are used in moderation
- present or past tense may be used

From *Iron Butterfly*, a romantic narrative by Claire Edward

The Choice: Jessica Gray is torn between her feelings for her old boyfriend, 'bad boy' surfer, Matt, who has already two-timed her with 'bikini girl', and her new boyfriend, Peter, who is reliable and devoted to her. Which one should she choose?

Content is suitable for older teens

'I'll pick you up at eight,' Peter whispered in Jess's ear. He squeezed her arm gently and walked off towards his car ...

Opens with dialogue

The Surf Club was transformed into a nightclub with swirling lights. It was packed with local surfers. Most of the guys were looking uncomfortable in black tie outfits, like they'd rather be in board shorts, barefoot, with their feet in the water. Jess's heart jumped when she spotted Matt leaning against the wall, alone, in the far corner of the room, devastatingly handsome in his dinner suit. He was staring at her. Was it in admiration? Jess knew she stood out in her low-cut, scarlet dress. Especially when Peter led her onto the dance floor.

Brief description creates visual effect/past tense/setting appeals to teen audience

It was impossible to speak over the music, so Jess didn't notice the punch coming. One minute, Peter was standing close to her, the next he was in a crumpled heap on the floor. He'd melted to the floor like a warm ice-cream, before she could reach her hand out to stop him, and before she could turn around to see what had happened.

Third person narrative seen through the eyes of the main protagonist, Jess

But there was no need for Jess to turn. Who else would the punch come from? Not only was Matt suddenly beside her, but he was obviously drunk. He swayed in front of her like one of the streamers that were beginning to detach themselves from the walls. Matt, too, was unattached. He looked so alone. No bikini girl. No mates. He opened his mouth, but no words came out. Instead he lurched towards her and vomited on her left shoe.

Use of question form to signify reflection of main character

Lucky they'd hired security for the night. A burly man in a dark uniform rushed over and escorted Matt to the door. The music stopped and everyone on the dance floor was staring from Jess to Matt to Pete, and whispering.

Strong dramatic action features in this incident

Pete grinned weakly at her as he rose from the floor. Someone in the crowd passed her a handful of paper napkins. She removed her silver shoe and wiped it carefully, trying not to breathe in the mingled smell of alcohol and vomit.

Attention to detail/contrasting personalities of male characters shown

'C'mon', she whispered to Pete. 'Let's get out of here.' The last thing she saw was the security guard pushing Matt into a taxi. Matt's reflection in the back window showed that he had sobered up enough to realise that he'd 'stuffed up'. He gave Jess a sad little smile. She turned away quickly. Could she bring herself to forgive him again?

Uncertain chapter ending creates suspense

1 Definition

Speculative fiction is a **generic** term for fantasy, science fiction and historical fiction.

2 Purpose and role of writer

To entertain; to 'suspend disbelief' by convincing the reader that such a world could exist

3 Generic features

Structure and organisation

- plot comprises: orientation, complication, **resolution**
- plot: often a quest, a journey, a problem to solve or enemy to defeat, e.g. *wars against the sea slugs*
- theme: often the battle of good and evil forces
- early chapters: rising action including some minor crises, e.g. *'They're out there somewhere.'*
- early chapters: usually establish details about the imaginary world, e.g. *underwater world*
- the **climax**: the moment when the main character usually reaches a turning point
- characters: main character/hero/heroine and other minor characters, e.g. *Grandian/Calamari*
- setting: a definite place, time and social setting, e.g. *inky waters*
- multiple narrators possible

Language

- description of places, people, events, e.g. *pillars*; *battlements*; *tentacled*; *wars*
- dialogue between characters suits the type of world created, e.g. *'Right you are, Sir,'*
- action through the author or narrator's eyes
- reflection by the author or central character/s, e.g. *Secretly, he admires this man*
- vocabulary may be formal, colloquial, poetic, figurative, symbolic, old-fashioned

Grammar

- method of narration: first, second or third person, e.g. *He speaks out loud.*
- past or present tense, e.g. *Grandian exhales loudly*
- variety of short and long sentences

Will Calamari be a battered squid?

Title creates suspense and humour

Grandian rests a tentacle on one of the pillars of his battlements. His eyes bulge as he peers into the distance. But it's impossible to see through the inky waters. His squad of special service squid have made the area impenetrable to the naked eye. Grandian exhales loudly, blowing impatient bubbles that cause a coughing fit.

Creates visual imagery as well as suspense; gives an indication of plot direction through language choices; personifies the squid

'They're out there somewhere.' He speaks out loud. Then, picking up his conch shell, he blows loudly, summoning the leader of his warriors, General Calamari.

Sea setting is sustained; dialogue creates variety in the narrative

The general gives his customary double-tentacled salute.

Humour

'Yes, sir?' he inquires crisply.

'I think it's time to send a few of our slippery fish out to scout for the enemy, Calamari.' Grandian rests his shortest tentacle beneath his chin, and looks quizzically at the general. Secretly, he admires this man who has served him so well throughout his reign so far. Calamari has risked life and limbs, all of them, time and time again in the wars against the sea slugs. He'd been battered nearly to death in the last battle.

Plot development is typical of speculative fiction; character development; reflection

'Right you are, sir,' Calamari replies. 'The slugs are slow, but I hear on the current that they've enlisted the help of the giant southern sea horses. They could be here sooner than we think.'

Story advances through dialogue; mood of urgency; language of the sea

Grandian realises that there is no time to waste. He must protect his kingdom from the slime of the sea. Those sinister creatures cannot be trusted. 'Send out the 16 slipperiest fish we have. Have the Special Sea Service posted along all the borders. And, Calamari,' he pauses, and seems to deliberate, 'tell the SSS to use the secret weapon if necessary.'

Use of **sibilance** to reinforce humour; battle of good and evil is developing

'Do you really think that's necessary, Sir?'

'You heard me, Calamari. If the slugs are sighted in our territory, the Special Sea Service is to squirt the poisoned ink.'

Conclusion gives indication of future action; ending is left open

1 Definition

A news article is an account of the important news of the day.

2 Purpose and role of writer

To provide accurate facts about a specific event

3 Generic features

Structure and organisation

- headline: short, catchy or cleverly worded, summarises the angle of the article; use of alliteration or a play on words is a common device, e.g. *Orange Sky Laundry cleans up again*
- subheading: brief but provides more detail
- byline: the reporter's name
- inverted pyramid structure: important information first – major points to minor points; allows readers to skim read and permits editing quickly to meet a publishing deadline
- introduction (20–25 words): 5Ws and the 1H (i.e. who, what, where, when, why and how) as well as the angle/point of view of the article, e.g. *When Cyclone Debbie hit the central coast of Queensland last week ...*
- body of the article: factual details and quotes from witnesses or experts; short paragraphs for ease of reading, containing one main fact or idea, e.g. *One resident described the service as a 'godsend'.*
- conclusion: unimportant because the article may be shortened to fit into the newspaper at the last minute, e.g. *Orange Sky Laundry is funded by donations and manned by hundreds of volunteers.*
- written in column format
- a lead/front page or important article may have a photograph of the event

Language

- simple vocabulary
- clear factual writing
- use of third person
- concise and economical

Grammar

- short sentences
- short paragraphs
- third person/present/past tense, e.g. *... the laundry provided clean, dry and even folded washing ...*

Orange Sky Laundry cleans up again

In the wake of the devastation caused by Cyclone Debbie last week, enter Orange Sky Laundry

Catchy headline/clear angle

Chloe Jacobi reports
20 January 2017

When Cyclone Debbie hit the central coast of Queensland last week, Orange Sky Laundry was there to help. Founders, Nicholas Marchesi and Lucas Patchett, joined the band of helpers rushing to the stricken area. At first, it was just one van, manned by volunteers. Then the two teenagers decided to ramp up their laundry service for hundreds of residents without power. A hire company provided them with a bus that the two urban heroes fitted out with washers and dryers.

Short sentences

After battling floodwaters, the mobile laundry provided clean, dry and even folded washing to locals in Mackay and Airlie Beach. One resident described the service as a 'godsend'. Again, Marchesi and Patchett witnessed the chaos of flooded streets and fallen power lines. Back in 2015, they had travelled to North Queensland to help cyclone-affected residents get back on their feet.

Factual content

Orange Sky Laundry began in September 2014. Two teenagers doing something practical for the growing number of homeless people who sleep rough at night in the city; now their laundry service is an iconic sight there.

Background information

In 2016, after the success of their laundry service, Marchesi and Patchett were named Young Australians of the Year. Since then, they have expanded their service to other capital cities and regional centres from Hobart to Perth. Plans to expand the service to Darwin are on the drawing board.

Clean clothes are only part of the package. It's the conversations that take place between the disadvantaged and the volunteers that ensures the success of the service. This practical service has become much more. Human interaction has been the most positive spin-off for the local lads who just wanted to give back to their community. Orange Sky Laundry is funded by donations and manned by hundreds of volunteers. It is the only free laundry service in the world.

Present tense

1 Definition

A nonfiction text is a text that is factual or based on fact.

A nonfiction essay analyses and evaluates a nonfiction text in response to a set question

2 Purpose and role of writer

The purpose of nonfiction is to inform on a particular subject. The writer is generally some sort of expert in the field about which he/she is writing.

The purpose of a nonfiction essay is to analyse and evaluate a text relevantly and effectively.

3 Generic features

Structure and organisation

- Nonfiction is usually
  - written in chapters, e.g. *Each chapter creates an insight ...*
  - chronological in structure, e.g. *The book is arranged chronologically ...*
  - arranged according to subject matter
- Essays about nonfiction texts
  - follow the introduction/body/conclusion model of literary essays
  - have paragraphs that conform to a set format, with topic sentences, followed by examples, quotes from the nonfiction text and linking devices between paragraphs
  - use the introduction to respond to the question by posing a hypothesis
  - analyse a different aspect of the text in each paragraph

Language

- The language of nonfiction writing
  - may be formal or informal depending on the topic
  - may be specialist or generalist depending on the topic
- The language of essays about nonfiction
  - is formal and impersonal, e.g. *There have been a number of nonfiction books ...*
  - uses literary terms

Grammar

- The grammar used in nonfiction
  - depends on the topic of the text
  - may be written in first, second or third person, present or past tense
- The grammar used in essays on nonfiction
  - is conventional and correct, with complex sentences
  - is written in third person in a detached tone, e.g. *From reading* Unpolished Gem *it is clear ...*

Essay question: Reading about the experiences and lives of others, whether fictional or real life, can offer the reader new insights. Discuss this statement with reference to a nonfiction text you have studied.

There have been a number of nonfiction books written in the last 20 years about the experience of growing up in a new country, especially those written by members of families who have migrated to Australia. Alice Pung's *Unpolished Gem* is one such book. The author was born in Australia shortly after her Chinese parents and grandmother moved here from Cambodia. The book traces Pung's life, beginning from her childhood and working towards adulthood. Each chapter creates an insight into what it feels like to be part of an ethnic minority in Australia.

Introduction names title and author/provides background information and addresses the topic directly

The book is arranged chronologically as Alice matures. She has been renamed after the main character in Lewis Carroll's *Alice in Wonderland*, as this is how her family feel about their new country. Pung reports that her parents are overwhelmed by the generosity of the Brotherhood of St Laurence, which clothes them, and the government, which pays them benefits. The supermarkets are like a fairy land with their bright lights and displays. All this is told in the words of Alice's parents and grandmother: 'Next my grandmother says her version of grace. 'Ah, Buddha, bless our Father government,' she exults.' This technique makes the reader understand and empathise with the Chinese–Cambodian family and realise how different our backgrounds and expectations of life are to theirs.

Refers to structure/provides examples/uses quotes/effect of quotes on reader

From reading *Unpolished Gem*, it is clear that, even for Alice, being born in Australia did not make acceptance of her Chinese–Cambodian background by her peer group automatic. The Asian students at her high school clung together, never feeling as cool or clever as their white Australian counterparts. Alice reveals her insecurities in the book that led to her becoming an introvert and a nerd. She really was unhappy for a long time, partly because the values of her culture are so different from those of the majority.

Purpose of nonfiction/ examples of insights revealed

The reader also learns that Alice has a sense of humour, and can laugh at herself and her family. Incidents such as the rivalry for her affections between her mother and her grandmother, and the time her mother mistakenly served dog food to the family because she couldn't read the labels in the supermarket, are very funny. So are some of the members of Alice's extended family. The importance of family to Alice's culture is also a contrast with our own, as is their incredible work ethic.

This work ethic allowed Alice's parents to send her to a 'good' school, enabling her to study law at the University of Melbourne. And now there is Alice's book, another example of her success. Nonfiction, especially if it is told honestly and from the heart, can provide new and interesting insights for every reader.

Conclusion evaluates the book and refers back to the question

1 Definition

An essay on a novel demonstrates knowledge and insight into a literary text.

2 Purpose and role of writer

An academic essay that informs the reader by developing and proving a hypothesis in response to a set question

3 Generic features

Structure and organisation

- introduction: responds to the topic with relevant comments
- body: develops the hypothesis in a series of logically sequenced paragraphs
- conclusion: restates the hypothesis and sums up the argument with a final evaluative comment, e.g. *The end of the novel clarifies Golding's perspective further.*
- paragraph structure follows a set formula
  - topic sentences are the opening sentences of each paragraph, e.g. *However, Golding introduces a note of hope early in this dystopian novel ...*
  - the body of the paragraph is an explanation or elaboration of the general opening statement
  - each paragraph should then provide examples from the text being analysed, or a quote from the text
  - the final sentence is a **clincher** which concludes this aspect of the argument and provides a link to the next paragraph, e.g. *The reader is positioned to adopt Golding's theory that man is intrinsically evil.*

Language

- formal language
- literary terms, e.g. *futuristic setting*; *dystopian*
- linking words, e.g. *However*
- conclusive words, e.g. *Finally*

Grammar

- complex sentences
- paragraph structure
- quotations from the text, e.g. *'the darkness of man's heart'*
- third person
- present tense, e.g. *There is further irony ...*

Discuss how the author has attempted to position readers to his/her perspective in a novel you have studied.

In *Lord of the Flies* (1954), William Golding has created the futuristic setting of a nuclear war. His characters, a group of young boys, are stranded on a deserted island in the Pacific Ocean, and must fend for themselves until they are rescued. Golding shows how, in the absence of adult supervision, these boys revert progressively to primitive and uncivilised behaviour. The reader is positioned to adopt Golding's theory that man is intrinsically evil.

Originally written as a reaction to an earlier novel, *The Coral Island* (1858) by R.M. Ballantyne, a boy's own adventure type of story, *Lord of the Flies* counters the idea that Christianity and British values will win out over evil influences: 'We've got to have rules and obey them. After all, we're not savages. We're English, and the English are best at everything.' Ironically, the main perpetrator of savage behaviour in the novel is the character of Jack Merridew, who is leader of the school choir.

However, Golding introduces a note of hope early in this dystopian novel, when a sensible and optimistic boy named Ralph is named leader of the group. His focus is on survival and rescue, but he is ultimately unable to maintain control. Not only does his rescue fire die out due to lack of supervision, but the group is quickly drawn to Ralph's rival, the sinister Jack, who becomes the leader of the hunters, and represents food, as well as the fun of pursuing and killing the wild pigs that inhabit the island.

That the process of civilised behaviour is undermined, despite the influence of Ralph's leadership and his more mature and responsible allies, underlines Golding's perspective on human nature: 'The world, that understandable and lawful world, was slipping away.' Where Ballantyne's characters in *The Coral Island* meet with external dangers, Golding emphasises that evil comes from within, regardless of Christian values.

When the boys begin to fear a mythical beast, their behaviour descends into savagery, which leads to the death of two of the vulnerable, but well-intentioned boys. Fortunately, rescue occurs just as Ralph is being hunted like one of the island's pigs. There is further irony when the naval commander who rescues the boys is oblivious to their brutal behaviour. As Ralph collapses on the beach in front of his adult rescuer, he weeps 'for the end of innocence' and 'the darkness of man's heart'. Finally, the end of the novel clarifies Golding's perspective.

Introduction names title, date of publication and author of novel

Introduction responds to the essay topic directly, using the words of the question

Topic sentence signposts the content of the paragraph

Background information

Relevant quotes are used as evidence

Reference to plot and characters strengthens the response

Final sentence of a paragraph clinches the argument

Conclusion reinforces the argument

1 Definition

A play is a prose text, written in dialogue, designed to be performed and viewed rather than read. An essay about a play is a piece of literary criticism that analyses and evaluates the text.

2 Purpose and role of writer

The playwright aims to entertain and, perhaps, convey a point of view. The writer of a drama essay aims to provide insight into the play by responding to a set question in a relevant and literate manner.

3 Generic features

Structure and organisation

- introduction: names the text and its author and poses a hypothesis in response to a set question
- body: develops the hypothesis in a series of logically sequenced and relevant paragraphs
- conclusion: restates the hypothesis and sums up with a final evaluative comment, e.g. *Louis Nowra has created a remarkable play*
- paragraph structure follows a set formula:
  - topic sentences open each paragraph and signpost the argument, e.g. *Even from the outset ...*
  - the body of the paragraph explains and elaborates on the opening sentence
  - each paragraph should provide examples or a quote from the text, e.g. *'They need me,'*
  - the final sentence of the paragraph clinches the argument

Language

- formal language
- literary terms, e.g. *plot*; *dialogue*; *staging*
- linking words, e.g. *Even*; *also*
- conclusive words

Grammar

- complex sentences, e.g. *Set in a mental institution in the 1970s, during the Vietnam War ...*
- paragraph structure
- quotations from the text, e.g. *'normal people who have done extraordinary things'.*

Essay question: The purpose of a play is to entertain as well as to persuade an audience to a point of view. Discuss this statement with reference to a play you have studied.

Cosi by Louis Nowra is a modern Australian play that is both entertaining and persuasive. Set in a mental institution in the 1970s, during the era of the Vietnam War, *Cosi* entertains through humour and clever dialogue. It also persuades its audience on a number of issues related to mental illness and war.

> Introduction addresses the key words of the topic and provides general background information

Even from the outset, the plot of *Cosi* promises to be intriguing and suspenseful. Lewis Riley, a somewhat 'flaky' arts graduate, has been employed to stage a show in a mental institution with the patients as the actors. Most people find institutions, and the people confined in them, a source of interest, especially mental institutions that few members of the public ever visit. Lewis is more interested in a paying job than anything else, but it is clear that he has no idea of the difficulties he will encounter as the director of *Cosi fan Tutte*, the opera by Mozart.

> Topic sentence/central character/formal language and complex sentences
>
> Background information

It is Roy, one of the most eccentric of the patients, who insists on the staging of the opera. Like many of the patients, Roy is a long term inmate who is delusional but not insane. The inmates of the asylum are entertaining because of the variety of personalities represented and the way they interact. They range from introverts to drug addicts and include one pyromaniac who is obsessed with anything to do with sex. Justin, the resident social worker, describes the patients to Lewis at the beginning of the play as 'normal people who have done extraordinary things'.

> Other characters entertain and persuade/use of quotation

Lewis finds this assessment of the cast to be true. One of the messages of the play is about commitment. Lewis finds himself increasingly connected to the inmates in a way that he could not have anticipated. 'They need me,' he tells his girlfriend, Lucy, when he decides that the play is more important than protesting against the war in Vietnam. *Cosi fan Tutte* is about love and fidelity and these are values that Lewis learns to prize during Nowra's play

> Reference to the key word: persuade/use of quotation

The playwright also persuades us that people in mental institutions are not to be shunned or written off as worthless or emotionally incapable. Lewis does get involved with one of the young patients, Julie, an addict. Lewis's empathy is therapeutic for Julie and participating in the play distracts her from her fixation on drugs, just as it is an effective diversionary therapy for the other patients.

> Further reference to persuasion

Louis Nowra has created a remarkable play, full of wit and humour, with a likeable 'hero' and some thought-provoking issues.

> General conclusion

1 Definition

A play script is the text or written version of a play.

2 Purpose and role of writer

To entertain or to present a point of view about an issue or human nature in general

3 Generic features

Structure and organisation

- play script divided into scenes and acts
- written in dialogue, e.g. *Charming day it has been, Miss Fairfax.*
- stage directions included to describe movement, gesture, facial expression and interaction between characters, e.g. *[Nervously.]*; *[Glibly.]*
- plot involves conflict between and/or within characters, e.g. *But you don't really mean to say that you couldn't love me if my name wasn't Ernest?*
- number of characters restricted by stage performance
- physical setting also limited due to staging

Language

- dialogue to suit the social and cultural context of the play, characters' ages, genders, personalities, plus the social and historical setting/social and cultural context of the play, e.g. *... my ideal has always been to love some one of the name of Ernest.*
- language may include colloquialisms, slang, **expletives**

Grammar

- sentence fragments: emphasis on realism rather than grammatical correctness
- all tenses can be used
- first, second or third person

Delivery

- Be sure that you understand the plot, your character and relationships with others.
- Enunciate clearly, speak loudly if on a stage and be confident.
- **Apt** vocal expression is vital to becoming a convincing actor.
- Plan your movements and facial expression to match the text.

From Act 1 of *The Importance of Being Earnest* by Oscar Wilde

Jack. Charming day it has been, Miss Fairfax.

Formal dialogue indicates that the play is set in an earlier era

Gwendolen. Pray don't talk to me about the weather, Mr. Worthing. Whenever people talk to me about the weather, I always feel quite certain that they mean something else. And that makes me so nervous.

Jack. I do mean something else.

Gwendolen. I thought so. In fact, I am never wrong.

Jack. And I would like to be allowed to take advantage of Lady Bracknell's temporary absence …

Gwendolen. I would certainly advise you to do so. Mamma has a way of coming back suddenly into a room that I have often had to speak to her about.

Jack. [Nervously.] Miss Fairfax, ever since I met you I have admired you more than any girl … I have ever met since … I met you.

Stage directions and dialogue create insight into characters

Gwendolen. Yes, I am quite well aware of the fact. And I often wish that in public, at any rate, you had been more demonstrative. For me you have always had an irresistible fascination. Even before I met you I was far from indifferent to you. [**Jack** looks at her in amazement.] We live, as I hope you know, Mr. Worthing, in an age of ideals. The fact is constantly mentioned in the more expensive monthly magazines, and has reached the provincial pulpits, I am told; and my ideal has always been to love some one of the name of Ernest. There is something in that name that inspires absolute confidence. The moment Algernon first mentioned to me that he had a friend called Ernest, I knew I was destined to love you.

Jack. You really love me, Gwendolen?

Gwendolen. Passionately!

Jack. Darling! You don't know how happy you've made me.

Gwendolen. My own Ernest!

Jack. But you don't really mean to say that you couldn't love me if my name wasn't Ernest?

Introduction of a complication or conflict

Gwendolen. But your name is Ernest.

Jack. Yes, I know it is. But supposing it was something else? Do you mean to say you couldn't love me then?

Gwendolen. [Glibly.] Ah! that is clearly a metaphysical speculation, and like most metaphysical speculations has very little reference at all to the actual facts of real life, as we know them.

Formal language indicates that the play is not a contemporary one

Jack. Personally, darling, to speak quite candidly, I don't much care about the name of Ernest … I don't think the name suits me at all.

Gwendolen. It suits you perfectly. It is a divine name. It has a music of its own. It produces vibrations.

Extract ends on a note of suspense

1 Definition

An analysis of poetry demonstrates knowledge of, and insight into, a literary text.

2 Purpose and role of writer

An academic essay that informs the reader by developing and proving a hypothesis in response to a set question

3 Generic features

Structure and organisation

- introduction: names the text and its author and poses a hypothesis, e.g. *it creates clear pictures*
- body: develops the hypothesis in a series of logically sequenced paragraphs
- conclusion: restates the hypothesis and sums up with a final evaluative comment
- paragraph structure follows a set formula
  - topic sentences are the opening sentences of each paragraph, e.g. *The second stanza brings a change of mood.*
  - the body of the paragraph is an explanation or elaboration of the general opening statement
  - each paragraph should then provide examples from the text being analysed, or a quote from the text, e.g. *'planted sand'*, *'locked'*, *'confinement'*
  - final sentence: a clincher which concludes this aspect of the argument and provides a link to the next paragraph, e.g. *The scene has a sense of foreboding.*

Language

- formal language
- literary terms, e.g. *imagery, mood and contrast*
- figurative language, e.g. *planted sand* (**metaphor**); *like a neat village green* (**simile**)
- linking words, e.g. *contrasting*; *but it can also*
- conclusive words

Grammar

- complex sentences
- paragraph structure
- quotations from the text

Illawarra coastline

At Austinmer the **planted sand**
looks like a **neat village green**
locked between headlands.
The sea **ripples obediently** to the shore.
Even in the rock pools, the waves
in their **confinement, lave gently**.
Further south at Fairy Meadow
oily grey waves spew onto the shore,
licking the shore hungrily, pestering.
Retreating from the ocean's edge
I turn towards the **dark escarpment**
frowning over the beach at **high tide**.

Model answer

'Illawarra coastline' is an effective poem because it creates clear pictures in the reader's mind through the use of imagery, mood and contrast.

At Austinmer Beach, nature seems controlled by human action. 'Planted sand' is a metaphor suggesting human handiwork. The beach is flat and level, as seen in the simile 'like a neat village green', as if human hands have smoothed it and placed it neatly between two headlands. The words 'locked' and 'confinement' imply that the beach is imprisoned. The sea is tame here. 'Ripples' are small waves and 'lave' means to wash against the shore. The poet has created a feeling of serenity where nature is in harmony with people.

Theme of the poem clearly stated; figurative language is identified; individual words are isolated and their effect described; mood is described

The second stanza brings a change of mood. The beach at Fairy Meadow is wild and rough. It may be later in the day. The weather has changed as the tide has risen. This is no longer a picture of order and beauty. The water is not even clean. The waves are personified as a wild beast: 'spewing', 'licking' and 'pestering'. The poet has entered the poem and is feeling threatened. Even the backdrop to the scene, the escarpment, is personified as looking down on the beach angrily. Now the reader sees that nature's mood can change. The scene has a sense of foreboding.

Topic sentence establishes contrast; personal referents; **personification** of nature to create a threatening mood

In emphasising the differences between two beaches along this stretch of coast, and through the use of personification the poet gives Austinmer and Fairy Meadow contrasting 'personalities', showing that nature may appear tame, but it can also become wild and unpredictable.

Conclusion shows link between poet's purpose or theme and techniques used

1 Definition

A report is an informative text written in an impersonal style.

2 Purpose and role of writer

To inform or provide advice based on research undertaken on a specific topic

3 Generic features

Structure and organisation

- cover page outlining title of report
- contents page detailing each numbered section of the report
- introduction explains the rationale (reasons the report has been commissioned), its scope and the process by which information was obtained, e.g. *The road toll continues to be a source of concern …*
- body of the report outlines its findings in logical order
- conclusion makes general points as a result of the report and may include recommendations or solutions to problems discussed in the report, e.g. *Current restrictions on provisional drivers …*

Language

- formal English, e.g. *This could be related to location …*
- precise, factual and objective language, e.g. *Age: is the key factor.*
- use of statistics, e.g. *Indigenous youth are five times more likely to suffer injury or be killed behind the wheel.*

Grammar

- correct English
- complex sentences
- specialised terminology relating to the topic, e.g. *provisional drivers*; *driver fatigue*
- present tense, e.g. *… young people are more likely …*
- use of first person is inappropriate

Driving it home

A message to youth about safety and survival on the road, commissioned by the National Road Safety Committee

Rationale: The road toll continues to be a source of concern in all states of Australia. Young drivers are still at the greatest risk of being killed on our national roads.

Logical structure; clear explanation of purpose and **parameters** of the report

Introduction: There are various government and private organisations that monitor the road toll. Here are some of their findings.

Main factors causing youth road injuries and fatalities

Use of apt headings and logical numerical point structure

1.1 Age: is the key factor. From 17 to 25 years, young people are more likely to die an accidental death than from illness. Nearly half of these accidents are road-related pertaining to drivers and passengers alike, especially provisional drivers.

1.2 Gender: Female drivers between 17 and 25 do not generally speed as frequently as their male counterparts.

1.3 Ethnicity: Despite being a fraction of the overall population, Indigenous youth are five times more likely to suffer injury or be killed behind the wheel. This could be related to location as well, as most Indigenous youth are rural dwellers.

Complex sentences and formal language

1.4 Location: More rural youth are involved in fatal car accidents. This may be due to road quality and higher speed limits in remote areas. Other factors include driver fatigue, drink driving habits, which are not as effectively policed, plus the age and condition of motor vehicles. Socio-economic factors are at play here too. Youth who live in the lower income area of outer city suburbs are more vulnerable to road casualty.

Topic sentence substantiated by evidence

1.5 Speed: is the most common factor in youth road fatalities. While young drivers represent a small minority on the road, nearly a third of recorded fatalities involve youth and speed.

Use of statistics

Conclusion: Statistical research indicates that factors involved in youth road fatalities include: age, gender, ethnicity, location of accidents, speeding, substance abuse and emotional issues of the individual drivers.

Conclusion sums up basic general points

Recommendations: Current restrictions on provisional drivers re: speed allowed, the ban on night driving and the carriage of passengers could be extended beyond the current time frame. More driver education programs need to be put in place, especially in rural areas.

1 Definition

A research assignment investigates a problem or a question, by referring to a variety of informative sources.

2 Purpose and role of writer

To form a hypothesis and solve a problem or respond to a question by selecting and evaluating relevant information

3 Generic features

Structure and organisation

Plan: develop research questions

- key terms of the question? (WHAT?) e.g. *causes of World War I*
- key dates and places (WHEN? WHERE?) e.g. *1871*; *1914*; *France*
- key facts/events/examples/people? (WHAT? WHO? HOW?)
- key causes? (WHY?) e.g. *imperialism, nationalism, the arms race and a complex set of alliances between nations*
- key effects/results/changes? (WHAT?) e.g. *destabilising Europe*

Research and reflection

- take notes from a variety of **primary** and **secondary sources**
- reflect on the value of/organise this information according to the research questions above
- develop a hypothesis and state it clearly in your introduction, e.g. *background and immediate cause resulted in a 'war climate'*
- organise your information into logically developed paragraphs
- use topic sentences to signpost your argument, e.g. *Another factor*
- use direct and indirect quotes to support your argument.

Draft your response: in paragraphs using correct referencing of source material

Final copy: an edited/corrected draft with correctly set out reference list

Language

- formal English
- specialised language according to topic, e.g. *war climate*; *nationalism*; *imperialism*
- linking words, e.g. *However*; *Another*; *Thus*
- clear, precise, unbiased language

Grammar

- correct paragraphing and punctuation
- complex sentences
- third person only, e.g. *when war broke out, the ordinary man in the street*

Assignment Task: Outline the major causes of World War I

The causes of the outbreak of World War I in 1914 are many and varied. There were background and immediate causes of what is called the Great War or 'the war to end all wars'. These included imperialism, nationalism, the arms race and a complex set of alliances between nations. A number of small conflicts arose that created a war climate in the early part of the 20th century, making war seem inevitable.

Introduction states hypothesis 'many and varied', 'war inevitable'; mentions a relevant date; lists the many causes; uses terminology, e.g. 'war climate'

Nationalism means loyalty and pride in one's country. Coupe (1981) states that as far as World War I is concerned, 'the fundamental causes can be traced back as far as the French and Economic Revolutions and the growth of nationalism, colonialism and economic rivalry which came with them'. Britain ruled a vast empire in this Victorian era. Germany and Italy were both unified into nation states in 1871, and their nationalistic feelings grew from this historic moment. France's nationalism grew from revenge and bitterness over the province of Alsace-Lorraine, which Germany had taken by force in 1871. In the formerly powerful Austro-Hungarian Empire, there were many small ethnic groups that wanted self-determination, a chance to create their own separate nations.

Sample paragraph; body develops the causes in turn; opens with a clear topic sentence; references quotes; develops the topic

Another factor that escalated nationalistic tensions was the press. Lawrence (1986) states that newspapers became a form of propaganda that built up feelings of aggressive nationalism, termed 'jingoism', encouraging the population to feel that their nation was superior. Thus when war broke out, the ordinary man in the street was keen to enlist, even if he did not fully understand the conflict.

Sample paragraph; topic sentence uses a linking word; second reference is an indirect quote; final clincher sentence uses 'thus' to indicate a concluding point

The immediate cause of World War I, the assassination of the Austrian Archduke Franz Ferdinand by a Bosnian student, released a 'powder keg' of aggressive feelings that had been simmering, ready to explode. However, this was just the culmination of other factors and rivalries that had been destabilising Europe for more than half a century.

Conclusion reinforces the original hypothesis; shows understanding of the topic; uses effective terminology and vocabulary

1 Definition

A documentary is a film that attempts to document reality, or a nonfiction film based on factual or real-life events.

2 Purpose and role of writer

To inform and comment on an event or issue

3 Generic features

Structure and organisation

- may be chronological, or based on aspects of an event or issue
- divided into scenes, e.g. *screen is divided*
- often features a presenter who 'leads' the audience through the experience
- may include interviews with experts or member of the public, e.g. *'a real madness in his eyes'*

Language

- language related to the topic
- informal language if interviews are used, e.g. *'It was wonderful'*
- use of facts and statistics, e.g. *on the tightrope for 45 minutes*
- may use voiceover
- may use persuasive language
- may use subtitles

Grammar

- spoken language, may be formal or informal
- sentence fragments
- may be past or present tense

This article about *Man on Wire* analyses and comments on features of the documentary genre

Not many documentaries have gained the notoriety that *Man on Wire* has achieved. This is due to the legendary and gripping story of Frenchman Philippe Petit's audacious walk on a tightrope between the Twin Towers in New York on 7 August 1974. The director, James Marsh, has ticked all the boxes for a fascinating insight into how this bold, history-making prank was achieved in his award-winning 2008 documentary film.

Introduction provides background information/director named

The 134-minute documentary gives the viewer more than just a brief skywalk (and back) between two famous buildings. It provides background into Petit's passion for tightrope walking, showing him practising at an early age with his girlfriend. The actual sky walk on the famous day is detailed from the moment Petit and his team entered the south tower disguised as workmen on the previous day. This is an elaborate procedure, made difficult by being a secret illegal mission.

A mixture of fact and opinion/use of statistics/background information

Also, the viewer is given an insight into the mind of Petit as he provides some of his own commentary in the documentary. 'If I die: what a beautiful deal – to die in the exercise of your passion.' This is his attitude to his dangerous lifestyle. There are also interviews and voiceover comments featuring his team and some of his friends.

Detail/use of adjectives

One comment describes him as having 'a real madness in his eyes'. Other people defend his walk between the two towers with comments like it was 'against the law, but not wicked or mean. It was wonderful'. However, the clandestine nature of Petit's quest creates an atmosphere of excitement and suspense, even though the viewer knows the outcome.

Quotations

Another technique that keeps the viewer interested is the camerawork. At times, the screen is divided to tell two stories. The left-hand side shows the ongoing story of the walk across the two towers, while the right-hand side shows Petit as a child, sometimes using a child actor to re-enact these scenes. The screen alternates between black-and-white and colour photography. The most spectacular shots are those that show Petit as a tiny man on a thin rope, surrounded by sky, walking, kneeling, lying and bouncing on the tightrope for 45 minutes. At the end of the stunt he was arrested by police.

Other techniques/opinionative language/terms related to the genre/descriptive language

Man on Wire is based on Philippe Petit's autobiography, *To Reach the Clouds*. It won awards at the 2008 Sundance Film Festival and in 2009 won a BAFTA for an 'Outstanding British Film' and an Academy Award for 'Best Documentary'.

Background information/general conclusion

1 Definition

A review is an analysis or appreciation of the quality of a film.

2 Purpose and role of writer

To inform and persuade/criticise

3 Generic features

Structure and organisation

- introduction
  - should include title and director and main actors
  - needs an angle/general opinionative comment, e.g. *will become a classic in Australian film history*
- brief plot analysis, e.g. *Samson and Delilah live unsatisfactory lives*
- ending not revealed, e.g. *there is some hope*
- analysis of key aspects of the film in a paragraph for each
  - key narrative techniques include: theme, plot, genre, characters, setting
  - key film features include: camerawork, acting, dialogue
  - include opinions on the quality of these aspects, e.g. *it screams* **authenticity**
- use key quotes from the dialogue
- provide some background on the director and the origin of the film
- make comparisons with other films by the director or in the same genre
- write in columns, in detail according to the word limit

Language

- formal
- literary and film language, e.g. *close-up shots*; *lack of dialogue*
- informative and opinionative, e.g. *won the 2009 Camera d'Or*; *a memorable film*
- impersonal language is the safe option, but reviewer may address reader, e.g. *Like me*

Grammar

- correct English is expected most of the time
- sentence fragments may be used for emphasis
- first person is optional, but should be limited to one or two comments
- present tense creates more immediacy

Film review: *Samson and Delilah*

Despite its Biblical title, or perhaps because of it, *Samson and Delilah* will become a classic in Australian film history. Firstly, it has the imprimatur of the Cannes Film Festival, where Warwick Thornton won the 2009 Camera d'Or award for best first feature film. Secondly, as the work of an Indigenous director, it screams authenticity.

Strong opinionative comments supported by facts

Samson and Delilah live unsatisfactory lives in the same remote community. Samson sniffs petrol and is plagued by the sounds of his brothers' music group, which plays outside his room all day. Delilah lives with her grandmother. As a result of her grandmother's death, Delilah finds herself in a stolen car, running away with Samson to Alice Springs. Delilah's quest is to cure Samson of his addiction, but there are many obstacles in the way.

Outlines plot briefly

Actors Rowan McNamara and Marissa Gibson are totally convincing as the aimless teenage boy and his more mature and focused girlfriend. The way Samson tries to attract Delilah's attention at the beginning of the film is entertaining and her growing dedication to him is impressive. Close-up shots of the two reveal the desperate face of the addict and helplessness of the supporter. The lack of dialogue in the film also adds to the emotional impact for the viewer.

Comments on quality of the acting and how the use of film techniques affect the viewer

The outback setting of Central Australia showcases the breathtaking beauty of the desert scenery as well as its isolation. This is offset by the poverty of the Aboriginal dwellings and the monotony of their existence. It is a relief when Samson and Delilah escape, though the town poses unforeseen challenges for both of them.

Setting and cinematography are evaluated

As in other recent films about Indigenous Australians, the perennial issues that plague Indigenous communities, such as poverty, substance abuse, lack of responsible males and lack of a future, are all evident here. And while there is no guarantee of redemption or improvement, there is some hope at the end of the film. Director Warwick Thornton has described his film as a love story, but it is much more than this. Like me, you will find *Samson and Delilah* a memorable film, disturbing and heart-wrenching, from a new and talented director.

Conclusion focuses on the film's purpose, and makes an overall assessment of its success

Andrea Jewel

1 Definition

A media article to present or promote the live performance of a text.

2 Purpose and role of writer

To inform and persuade. This is a public text.

3 Generic features

Structure and organisation

- use of headline and byline, e.g. *Today's Stolen Generation: Fact or Fantasy*
- brief plot outline
- establishment of the historical and social context of the play, e.g. *Set during the notorious times of the Stolen Generations, from 1910 to 1970 ...*
- written in columns

Language

- formal, literary language, e.g. *This version of our anthem distinguishes the gap between the Indigenous and non-Indigenous ...*
- use of key quotes from the play, e.g. *'You're one of us, Anne – we've brought you up as one of our own.'*
- informative and opinionative

Grammar

- use of third person, e.g. *Harrison explores the issues of racism and loss of identity.*
- formal English
- may use inclusive pronouns, e.g. *We are invited ...*
- present tense

Today's Stolen Generation: Fact or Fantasy?

Jane Harrison's play *Stolen* identifies the gap between the Indigenous and non-Indigenous citizens in our society, forcing us to confront the agendas whittling away our national identity

Subheading provides the angle of the text

Australians all let us rejoice, in snatching children from their mother's hands. We've golden soil and wealth for toil, where our Indigenous population is treated as second-rate citizens. Our land abounds in nature's gifts, which are only available to the select few. In history's page, let every stage ignore our mistreatment of First Nation peoples. In joyful strains then let us sing, Advance Australia Fair.

Introduction raises issue in the play

This reimagined version of our anthem distinguishes the gap between the Indigenous and non-Indigenous, a theme that continues to dictate our country today. This issue is explored in Jane Harrison's play *Stolen*, to be performed in the up-coming Australian Festival of Drama. Set during the notorious times of the Stolen Generations, from 1910 to 1970, the play focuses on five separate situations involving children in this era.

Background information and plot details

Harrison explores the issues of racism and loss of identity. The underpinning theme is the gap between Indigenous and non-Indigenous, which is still a feature of today's society.

We are invited to identify white people as cruel and heartless, seeking to abuse their innocent victims. Recent statistics show that over 70 per cent of secondary school students (including Aboriginal students) have experienced racism, a staggering figure considering our supposed national identity of 'mateship'.

Inclusive pronouns are persuasive

But, back to the play! Loss of identity is evident in *Stolen*, especially in the character of Anne. Unlike the other four children, Anne has been adopted and brought up in a loving white family. However, she finds out that her Indigenous parents are alive and want to claim her. Anne is torn between the two cultures. Her white father says, 'You're one of us, Anne – we've brought you up as one of our own,' and the black voice responds, 'But we're your real family. It's where you belong, girl.' Quite a dilemma for a confused young person.

Refers specifically to the text with apt quotes

Through *Stolen*, Jane Harrison has shown the torment and insecurity suffered in the past, due to ignorance and white assumptions of racial superiority to amend past errors, so that all Australians can advance in this fair land.

Reiterates central issues

Neat conclusion to promote the play

David Oates

1 Definition

Shakespearean drama refers to the plays written by the English dramatist and poet William Shakespeare (1564–1616). Shakespeare is regarded as the world's greatest playwright. His 37 plays include comedies, histories and, most famously, tragedies.

2 Purpose and role of writer

To entertain/to present a message about human nature

3 Generic features

Structure and organisation

- divided into five acts
- each act is subdivided into scenes
- first two acts represent the rising action of the play
- third act generally represents a turning point in the plot
- final acts represent the falling action leading to the resolution
- written in dialogue with few stage directions
- Shakespeare's plays generally feature characters of noble birth
- in tragedy, the central character – the tragic hero – is a man of virtue who, according to some scholars, contains a fatal flaw that leads to his downfall
- the plot involves the reversal of his fortune, leading to his downfall.
- the play often features supernatural forces – ghosts or witches – that influence the plot

Language

- written in **blank verse**, arranged in lines of poetry
- Shakespeare is most famous for his metaphorical language
- some of the language is dated and difficult to understand
- most famous speeches are the soliloquies, in which the character is alone on stage expressing his feelings in monologue form

Grammar

- play written in sentences but in stanza form

Analysing Hamlet's soliloquy

***Hamlet* is a Shakespearean tragedy about a Danish prince, who discovers that his uncle, Claudius, has murdered his father, the king, and married his mother, Gertrude. The ghost of the dead king swears Hamlet to avenge his death.**

A soliloquy is a speech or monologue, delivered by the character when he is alone on stage. Its purpose is to reveal the character's thoughts and feelings, and to give some indication of the future action of the play. Below is Hamlet's fifth soliloquy.

Act III, Scene 2

Hamlet: Tis now the very witching time of night, ········ Reference to the supernatural
When churchyards yawn and hell itself breathes out ········ Personification
Contagion to this world: now could I drink hot blood, ········ Metaphor
And do such bitter business as the day ········ Alliteration
Would quake to look on. Soft! now to my mother.
O heart, lose not thy nature; let not ever
The soul of Nero enter this firm bosom: ········ Reference to ancient Roman history
Let me be cruel, not unnatural:
I will speak daggers to her, but use none; ········ Metaphor
My tongue and soul in this be hypocrites; ········ Personification
How in my words so ever she be shent, ········ Rhyming couplet
To give them seals never, my soul, consent.

Hamlet is reacting to the confirmation that his uncle is guilty of his father's murder. He is angry with Claudius and extremely revengeful. This is evident in the line 'now could I drink hot blood', an exaggerated example of the way Hamlet feels, which creates a dramatic atmosphere in the play.

The seven soliloquies that Hamlet delivers in the play are varied in tone and intent. This is evidence of his instability as a result of his father's death and mother's remarriage. Here Hamlet also expresses his revulsion for his mother, in her betrayal of his father's memory. He has been summoned to his mother's room to be rebuked for his behaviour. Instead, Hamlet will 'speak daggers' to Gertrude. Tempted though he is, he will not harm her physically.

The theme of this speech is revenge. Shakespeare emphasises Hamlet's outrage and sense of duty to his father. He achieves this through metaphorical language and blank verse that create an atmosphere of tension and foreboding. As with most soliloquies, the final rhyming couplet creates a neat ending.

1 Definition

An essay on Shakespearean drama demonstrates knowledge of, and insight into, a literary text.

2 Purpose and role of writer

To write an academic essay that informs the reader by developing and proving a hypothesis in response to a set question

3 Generic features

Structure and organisation

- introduction: names the text and its author and poses a hypothesis, e.g. *Shakespeare's* Hamlet *conforms closely*
- body: develops the hypothesis in a series of logically sequenced paragraphs
- conclusion: restates the hypothesis and sums up with a final evaluative comment, e.g. *Thus,* Hamlet ...
- paragraph structure follows a set formula:
  - topic sentences are the opening sentences of each paragraph, e.g. *Shakespeare is famous*
  - the body of the paragraph is an explanation or elaboration of the general opening statement
  - each paragraph should then provide examples from the text being analysed, or a quote from the text, e.g. *Claudius, the wicked uncle, contrasts with his brother*
  - the final sentence is a clincher that concludes this aspect of the argument and provides a link to the next paragraph

Language

- formal language
- literary terms, e.g. *blank verse*
- linking words
- conclusive words, e.g. *However*; *Therefore*

Grammar

- complex sentences
- paragraph structure
- quotations from the text, e.g. *'O that this too too solid flesh would melt'*

Essay question: Discuss the ways in which the play *Hamlet* conforms to the general characteristics of Shakespearean tragedy.

Shakespeare's *Hamlet* conforms closely to the characteristics of Shakespearean tragedy, being written in blank verse, with a plot that traces a noble family and the reversal of fortune of the once noble hero. The plot juxtaposes good and evil characters – some of whom are supernatural – and has a message for people of all ages.

Introduction responds directly to the question by forming a hypothesis that develops four characteristics of the tragedy

Generally the audience of a Shakespearean play empathises with the protagonist. Hamlet is a character of noble birth and admirable qualities; until fate deals him a blow which changes his life forever. The audience admires Hamlet's sense of duty to his father when he swears to avenge his murder. However, the audience also becomes impatient, as Hamlet seems incapable of fulfilling this pledge.

Develops one of the four aspects outlined in the introduction, i.e. shows the two sides of the tragic hero that lead to his downfall

Although Shakespeare never travelled outside England, some of his plays are set abroad. *Hamlet* is set in Elsinore, Denmark, and the characters are the Danish royal family. This does not mean that all are virtuous characters. Claudius, the wicked uncle, contrasts with his brother, the late king. Gertrude, the queen, has been represented as a weak character. Hamlet is very melancholy and indecisive: 'O that this too too solid flesh would melt'.

Develops a second aspect, i.e. noble birth

Shakespeare is famous for the timelessness and universality of his plays. Although his plots are dramatic and sometimes lacking realism, the characters in his plays display complex human traits that are recognisable today, like ambition and vengeance. Hamlet describes his uncle as a 'remorseless, lecherous, treacherous villain'.

Develops a third aspect, i.e. universality; uses quote

The plots of Shakespeare's tragedies also follow a general pattern. The action in the first half of the play tends to be hopeful, despite some calamity. The tragic hero seems to be in control. The climax or turning point changes the fortunes of the protagonist. In *Hamlet*, the confirmation of Claudius's guilt comes via a play within the play, called *The Mousetrap*. From this point, Hamlet loses control of the action, thus allowing further tragedy to ocur. At the end of the play, all major characters are dead as a result of 'carnal, bloody and unnatural acts'.

Develops a fourth aspect, i.e. plot

There are some characteristics of Shakespearean tragedy that are less believable in modern society – the presence of the supernatural, for example. It is the ghost of Hamlet's father who reveals the murder plot. Four hundred years ago, the people of Shakespeare's time believed in supernatural phenomena. Today, we are not so superstitious. Nor are we used to plays written in poetic form. Shakespeare wrote his plays in blank verse with liberal use of metaphorical language.

Introduces other minor aspects

Thus, *Hamlet* is typical of other Shakespearean tragedies, being the story of a potentially great man undermined by circumstance. Although the main character dies, there is always one character left to take over the kingdom and restore order. Therefore, the tragedy ends on a positive note.

1 Definition

A short story is a narrative of less than 20 000 words with a simple plot, a small number of characters and a single setting. A short story can be read at one sitting.

2 Purpose and role of writer

To entertain

3 Generic features

Structure and organisation

- decide on a topic
- decide on a sub-genre: crime, fantasy, mainstream narrative
- decide on the angle or theme, e.g. *case of mistaken identity*
- decide on an appealing title
- plot the story with conflict, a series of crises, a climax and a conclusion
- aim to create atmosphere through suspense
- conclusion may be a twist or unexpected ending, e.g. *This was her final rehearsal*
- decide whether the story will have a traditional or alternative structure
- create characters: central character and one or two others, if necessary
- decide on a setting, e.g. *They continued to sit in the semi-darkness*
- decide on first, second or third person method of narration, e.g. *She*

Language

- language to suit the genre, era and social context of the story, as well as audience
- a blend of action, description, dialogue and reflection to create variety. This story has deliberately avoided using dialogue to create an atmosphere of silence and mystery.
- evocative language to create atmosphere, e.g. *She swallowed nervously*
- figurative language in descriptions, e.g. *Like shadows or slinky cats*

Grammar

- a variety of short and long sentences
- short sentences/fragments used for drama and impact
- a variety of sentence beginnings
- the correct conventions for writing dialogue
- correct paragraphing
- past or present tense e.g. past tense for past events

Sometimes silence says it all

No one spoke. They continued to sit in the semi-darkness, watching. Sitting on the dusty floor, all were dressed in black. Some of the girls had taken the blackness to extremes, Sarah noted, dyeing their hair and wearing black stockings that disappeared up their slim legs under their short skirts. They were all emaciated-looking, even the boys. It went with the territory. Like shadows or slinky cats, they moved around the room when they were summoned to take their turn.

Looking around restlessly, Sarah saw a tiny black spider weaving its web between the tattered curtains close to the narrow window at the side of the room. Like everything else in the cold building, the window was grimy. Outside, it was starting to drizzle and the sky was darkening prematurely. Sarah wished that she could slip through one of the cracks in the window unnoticed, even though it would be chilly outside.

It wasn't the silence that bothered her any more. She'd grown accustomed to reading facial expressions and the mood of the others' movements. To speak, even to whisper to Maura, the girl beside her, the redheaded girl with the freckles that looked like chocolate chips on her pale face, would be unforgivable. Sarah noticed that Maura was chewing her fingernails and staring blankly ahead. Must be psyching herself up.

Who could have imagined a group of teenagers could sit so silently and so still? They'd certainly learnt some discipline lately. It was like being reprogrammed, becoming robotic. To speak would be like laughing out loud in church. She shuddered at the thought.

Pulling the dark shawl closer to her chest, Sarah fixed her eyes on the pale young man in front of her. He was edging his way along the side wall as if he too wanted to escape through the nearby exit. His movements were furtive but fluid, like a dancer performing to some distant music that only he could hear. Then he melted back into the group, seating himself silently.

Suddenly Sarah was beckoned forward. She swallowed nervously, hiding her shaking hands behind her back. By the time she reached the front of the room, she felt her nerves begin to calm. It wasn't as if she had to remember any lines. There was no need to speak. It was movement and facial expression that were crucial. This was her final rehearsal at the famous Marcel Marceau School of Mime, and Sarah was about to give the most important performance of her acting career. She began her well-practised routine. Conscious that all the eyes in the room were upon her, Sarah enveloped herself in the silence, pleased that the ordeal would soon be over. No one spoke.

Title hints at the content of the story

Introduces other minor aspects

Introduction sets the scene visually and identifies the main character and the action/ language creates atmosphere

Focus on the main character

Third person narrative looks through main character's eyes/ becomes reflective

Use of rhetorical question/ emphasis on atmosphere

Verbs and adjectives create visual images of the scene/ figurative language

Story approaches climax and revelation of purpose as it focuses on the central character

Final sentence is a repetition of the opening

1 Definition

A song is a poem that can be sung.

2 Purpose and role of writer

To entertain or to arouse an emotional reaction

3 Generic features

Structure and organisation

- topic: is often love or relationships
- theme: is often sad about lost or unrequited love
- title: sums up the message of the song
- structure: stanza form, usually with a chorus
- generally regular stanza length; quatrains are common

Language

- emotive words, e.g. *alone*; *haunts*; *faithful*
- language creates dramatic atmosphere
- figurative devices like those used in poetry:
  - simile, e.g. *My life's like a nightmare*
  - metaphor, e.g. *The world is your oyster/Let me be your pearl*
- question form, e.g. *Why can't you love me?/Why won't you stay?*
- rhyme: regular rhyme scheme, e.g. *name/same*; *away/day*

Grammar

- written in lines, but in sentence form
- line divisions indicate pauses and create rhythm
- punctuation is used according to sentence division
- syntax (word order) may be varied as in poetry

Love whisper

When I'm alone I whisper your name
I still can't believe you don't feel the same
The love that we shared: it won't fade away
I know I'll love you, till my dying day

Emotive, personal language/ use of first person

My life's like a nightmare
that haunts me each day
Why can't you love me?
Why won't you stay?

Simile/dramatic mood/ question form

The world is your oyster
Let me be your pearl
I'll always be faithful
Your one and only girl

Metaphors

All I want is a chance
to prove that I can
love you forever;
you don't understand

Emotive language

Let bygones be bygones
Let's start anew – please!
You know I still want you
You know I'll be true

Repetition of words

Remember the good times
the love we both shared?
Those halcyon days
when you showed that you cared.

Development of emotional mood

I'm writing this letter
please listen to me
I've tried and I've tried
but I can't shake you free

When I'm alone I whisper your name
I still can't believe you don't feel the same
The love that we shared: it won't fade away
I know I will love you, love you, love YOU!
Till my dying day.

Repetition of chorus as the song builds to an emotional crescendo

1 Definition

A long dramatic speech by a character in a play, generally alone on stage.

2 Purpose and role of writer

To reveal the personality of the speaker, due to some inner conflict, or in response to a situation or series of events

3 Generic features

Structure and organisation

- written in play script form
- character alone on stage
- written in dialogue, e.g. *I see the blood again.*
- script may use stage directions, e.g. (Stabs herself)
- narrative structure, showing development of plot or personality, leading to some sort of climax or resolution

Language

- dialogue to represent the character and role of the speaker and the situation, e.g. *I did not wield the knife myself, but I'm responsible for their deaths.*
- language may be informal, emotive, persuasive
- imagery/personification may be used to create mood, e.g. *Death invites me*

Grammar

- use of first person
- present or past tense
- sentence fragments, e.g. *The things I made him do*

Delivery

- Voice should reflect text of monologue
- Tone should arouse emotional response in the audience
- Gesture should suit text and tone, e.g. (Confused, staring at her hands)
- Movement should complement gesture and text, e.g. (Moves to the window, leans forward)

Lady Macbeth: (*Confused, staring at her hands*) I see the blood again. Am I losing my mind? The blood Macbeth and I have shed has stained my hands and my soul. The things I made him do. (*Falls to her knees*) I must be mad. I must be evil.

At the beginning, I thrived on these deeds. (*Looks upwards, indicating remorse*) Then why do I feel so empty? If I'm evil, I should be punished. My blood should be spilled, just as the blood of Duncan, and his servants, and Banquo, and so many others. (*Lies down, one hand on her forehead, the other over her heart*) I may not have taken their lives. I did not wield the knife myself, but I'm responsible for their deaths. (*Gets up, paces, disillusioned*) Who is left? Only me and my deranged husband. Duncan is dead. Banquo is buried. Donalbain and Malcolm have been driven away.

What's done cannot be undone. (*Stands still, reflecting*) It's too late. I may not have held the dagger myself but I goaded my lord. I made him do it. I set him on the path. And to what? Honour? No … To destruction! What is there that's worth living for? I'm the Queen of Scotland, but life is futile. So much blood. The blood of mothers, the blood of wives and children. Did I shed this blood? No, it was him – my husband.

Where is the king? (*Goes to the door, looks out*) What is he plotting next? Is he consorting with those witches – if they even exist! He sees things. Banquo's ghost is haunting his troubled mind. I see things! The thanes fear us; they think we're tyrants. And we are tyrants.

Is this how my lord, Macbeth, sees us? I've always had the strength for both of us but now, he no longer listens. His mind is full of scorpions.

What's that? (*Moves to the window, leans forward*) The trees ... the trees are moving! I am going insane! The forest of Burnham is moving towards our castle. The witches' prophecy is coming true. Is that the cross of St George? It is coming to crush the cross of St Andrew! We're no longer safe!

I can't jump from here. They could capture me and my beloved Scotland would surely fall with me.

Wait! Is this a dagger I see before me? (*Stabs herself*) Another chance. Another way to go. I will take my life, as Macbeth did Duncan's. For justice, and for peace. I will redeem myself. God forgive me. Hell is murky. I go. (*Resolved, sinks slowly to the floor*) The time invites me. Death invites me. The rest is silence.

Adam Osborne, Year 12

Dramatic/personal

Background information

Imagery of blood and violence

First person pronouns

Imagery associated with mental instability

Question form indicates uncertainty

Conclusion brings resolution

1 Definition

An occasional speech is addressed to a specialised audience.

2 Purpose and role of writer

May be informative, social or persuasive, or purely entertaining

3 Generic features

Structure and organisation

- introduction should clarify purpose, e.g. *I want to encourage you ...*
- should hook the audience with a question or quote, e.g. *ask not ...*
- body of the speech should develop the text logically, with 'signposts' for listeners as well as examples or anecdotes
- conclusion should sum up and finish strongly, e.g. *Most importantly ...*
- leave the audience inspired or reflective, e.g. *Isn't that enough?*

Language

- language choice depends on context/occasion
- language should suit the topic and audience, e.g. *serve my community*; *work as a team*
- language should be sufficiently simple and clear to allow listeners to absorb the text

Grammar

- inclusive pronouns may be used
- short sentences and fragments for spoken purposes
- contractions for informality, e.g. *I'm*; *you'll*

Delivery:

- speak with conviction and sincerity
- enunciate carefully
- maintain eye contact
- stand still and limit gestures so audience is not distracted

Example

A famous American president once advised his fellow countrymen and women to 'ask not what your country can do for you – ask what you can do for our country.' Good morning students, and thank you for inviting me to your Senior School assembly. As Chairman of Pay It Forward, Australia, I want to encourage you to look beyond your school to see how you can contribute to your local community.

Original opening

What is the 'pay it forward' concept? It was immortalised in a film of the same name in 2000. A teacher assigns his class the task of coming up with an idea to improve the world and to put it in action. One student creates the philosophy of 'paying forward', doing a favour without expecting anything in return. Despite the risk to his safety, the boy's efforts are rewarded. Kindness begins to become contagious in his community.

Use of rhetorical questions

I'm not advocating risky behaviour, but I do recommend the film. I'm also going to suggest some strategies for you to consider. How can I serve my community, you ask, as well as attend school and fulfil my sporting and social commitments?

Well, you could combine the social aspects with the charitable ones. Work as a team with friends in some form of community service. Join the local branch of the State Emergency Service Cadets, or volunteer to pack food hampers at Foodbank. Match your community service to your interests – whether through sport, the environment, hospitality, working with kids or the elderly. There are endless choices of ways you can help.

Use of imperatives as a persuasive device

What's in it for me, you might be asking? Volunteering will connect you to your community, as well as teaching you practical and people skills. You'll gain empathy for people who have struggled through life to achieve what you probably take for granted. You'll gain maturity and a sense of civic responsibility. Most importantly, you will feel good about yourself. Isn't that enough?

Effective conclusion

1 Definition

A text-based speech analyses the issues and content of a text.

2 Purpose and role of writer/presenter

To show how texts can influence readers'/viewers' perceptions

3 Generic features

Structure and organisation

- opening should contain a **hook** to attract interest, e.g. *What's your passion?*
- introduction should contain a thesis, e.g. *It offers a team of like-minded players focused on a common goal.*
- body should develop the analysis logically with evidence
- topic sentences should signpost the analysis, e.g. *Director Clint Eastwood foreshadows the issues ...*
- conclusion should sum up the presenter's point of view

Language

- generally formal language, depending on topic and audience
- appeal to emotions and ideologies, e.g. *Is there something you love ...?*
- persuasive language, e.g. *also ensures the success ...*
- metalanguage, e.g. *foreshadows*; *feel good*; *casting ...*

Grammar

- may use inclusive pronouns, e.g. *you*, *your*
- may use first person
- usually delivered in present tense
- short sentences, or statements punctuated with pauses for ease of delivery
- rhetorical questions are effective

Delivery

- show conviction and sincerity
- enunciate carefully with vocal expression, pace and pause
- maintain eye contact
- stand still and limit gestures so audience is not distracted

Example

Good morning Students,

What's your passion? Is there something you love better than anything else in the world? Something you'd like to spend your whole life doing? I'm guessing for many of you, that your response will be sport – a code of football, perhaps.

Rhetorical questions to hook audience

Sport of any kind offers so much more than a ball and a uniform. It offers a team of like-minded players focused on a common goal. And that's what the film *Invictus* is about.

Thesis statement

Set in South Africa in 1994, at the end of the apartheid era, the film opens with Nelson Mandela being elected as the first black President of South Africa. He knows he has a mammoth challenge ahead of him, uniting a divided country of multicultural origins. How does he plan to achieve this? His strategy is to bring his people together via their national sport – rugby. And he plans to use the national team, the Springboks, to appeal to the patriotic and sporting spirit of the nation.

Background information

Director Clint Eastwood foreshadows the issues Mandela must deal with: the preference in the black population for soccer over rugby, and the racist attitudes of some whites, including the Springboks' coach and the team captain's family. In this 'feel good' movie, based on a novel entitled *Playing the Enemy* by Will Carlin, Nelson Mandela's charisma and devotion to his beloved South Africa are revealed.

The casting of actors Morgan Freeman and Matt Damon also ensures the success of the production. Both Eastwood, as director, and Freeman in the lead part won awards for their roles in the production. Freeman was outstanding in his representation of Mandela, capturing his quiet demeanour and the respect he commanded from his people.

Persuasive language

Another technique that is appealing to the viewer is the authentic footage of highlights of the World Cup Rugby series that led to the South African victory. The title of the film is also a source of inspiration. *Invictus* is a poem that Mandela gives to team captain, Francois Pienaar. It means 'unconquered' in Latin.

Analysis of film techniques

Nelson Mandela asserted that: 'Sport has the power to change the world. It has the power to inspire, the power to unite people that little else has ... It is more powerful than governments in breaking down racial barriers.' And in this case it seems he was right.

Use of imperative to create strong conclusion

1 Definition

A textual intervention is a creative response to a text, adding to the story or filling a gap or a silence.

2 Purpose and role of writer

To show an understanding of the content of the text which may recreate the style of the author

3 Generic features

Structure and organisation

- intervention is a prelude, interlude or postlude text, e.g. *The action takes place at the end of Chapter 1.*
- may conform to the original text in layout and development
- may be a chapter or a part of a chapter

Language

- may be consistent with the original text, e.g. *I like dogs because they don't talk and confuse me.*
- may show features of the original text, e.g. *The walls of the cell were blue*
- may use vocabulary consistent with the original text
- may be formal or informal, e.g. *I was in a cell at the police station*

Grammar

- may be first, second or third person, e.g. *I didn't feel tired. I wasn't even hungry.*
- may be present or past tense, e.g. *I liked being alone.*
- may be grammatically correct or not
- sentence fragments may be used

The following is a textual intervention based on the novel *The Curious Incident of the Dog in the Night-Time*, by Mark Haddon, about a boy with 'some behavioural difficulties'. The action takes place at the end of Chapter 1.

I was in the cell at the police station for 47 minutes and 23 seconds. I didn't know what would happen next so I sat down on the padded bench and waited.

Use of statistics and detail to show character's precise nature

The walls of the cell were blue, with some large white chips out of the paintwork near the floor. It looked like someone had kicked the wall because there were shoe marks there too. It reminded me of the sky and the clouds because of the colours. My teacher would probably ask me to write a simile about it, if she was in the room. But I don't like similes. I don't understand them, especially the really weird ones in the poetry we sometimes read. I don't like poetry. I like nonfiction books with lots of facts. But because the sky is blue on a fine day, I felt comfortable in the police cell.

I liked being alone. It gave me plenty of time to think about what had happened. I know that Mrs Shears called the police. She thinks I killed Wellington. I know that now because when she came out onto the front lawn in her pyjamas, I was holding on to Wellington and she swore at me. So many times, people don't understand me. I was trying to save Wellington. But it was too late. He was already dead. Like my mother.

Reference to solitary nature of character

Mrs Shears knows I like Wellington. Dogs are a lot more intelligent than some people. I like dogs because they don't talk and confuse me. I don't like people touching me, but I don't mind dogs jumping up on me because I know that means they want to be patted. When people touch me, I don't know what they want. That's why I hit the policeman. That's why I'm sitting here.

First person, past tense/ reflection on past events to orientate the reader

It was nice and cool in the police cell. At 12.34, one of the officers looked in at me. He opened the hatch and nodded. I didn't know what that meant so I ignored him. I didn't feel tired. I like night-time because it's quiet and everyone else is in bed. I wasn't even hungry. I thought about my pet rat, Toby. I wondered if he was asleep. If he was awake, he would be hungry. I always give him a snack before I put him into his cage at night.

Shows knowledge of character's feelings and **emotional detachment**

I was just thinking about how the room was perfectly symmetrical when I heard voices. Nobody came, so I started to think about the death of Wellington. When I get home I am going to make a list of suspects and a plan for how I will solve the crime. Then Mrs Shears will be pleased. Mrs Shears knows I always tell the truth. She didn't ask me if I knew who killed Wellington, so I didn't tell her. I will find out for her, for Wellington really. Then if Mrs Shears gets another dog, she will let me take him for a walk.

Sentence structure use of 'I' to show character's self-centredness

'What the bloody hell's going on?' I recognised that voice echoing down the corridor. Father had finally arrived.

Ends on a note of suspense

1 Definition

A textual reconstruction changes or reconstructs some aspect/s of a text, often in a different genre.

2 Purpose and role of writer

To show an understanding of a text by responding to it creatively, generally reinforcing, but sometimes **resisting**, the meaning of the original text

3 Generic features

Structure and organisation

- choose a part of the text where the story can be reconstructed
- choose an appropriate genre for the reconstruction, e.g. narrative, feature article
- if the narrative genre is used, there should be a balance of action, narrative, dialogue, description and reflection, e.g. *Now he feels vulnerable*
- a reconstruction can be a fragment or episode, a 'small picture'; does not have to cover the whole text, e.g. The text ends abruptly as the doctor arrives.

Language

- must suit the plot, characters and setting of your reconstruction
- may vary from formal to informal, depending on its purpose, e.g. *'So, who's this Dr Freud, anyway?'*
- should suit the chosen genre

Grammar

- consistent person and tense throughout the text, e.g. third person: *Hamlet*; *he*
- apply the rules of narrative writing or the genre chosen to the text; refer to the rules that apply to other text types elsewhere in this writing guide

This textual reconstruction has transformed *Hamlet* by William Shakespeare into a modern setting. Hamlet has been acting strangely since his father's mysterious death and his mother's remarriage to an uncle whom he detests. Is Hamlet mad or sad? To find out, his mother plans to have him see a psychologist.

'What's this?' Hamlet bursts into his mother's room without knocking. He's holding a piece of paper in his hand. — Dialogue creates mood, establishes modern setting, begins plot

'It's a referral, Hamlet, to a specialist. I made the appointment for you,' his mother, Gertrude, replies, startled by his abrupt and noisy entry. She's sitting in her favourite chair by the window, reading. Now she places her book on the window ledge. — Establishes setting, creating visual effect

'So who's this Dr Freud anyway?' Hamlet paces across the room restlessly as Gertrude watches him closely. — Insight into character

'He's an eminent psychologist, Hamlet,' Gertrude replies, an anxious tone in her voice. 'You need a doctor. You're sick, even if you don't realise it.' — Creates mood

'Sick? What am I suffering from?' Hamlet's voice rises in anger. He turns to face her. 'Well?' — Creates conflict, suspense

Gertrude stands and moves towards him warily. She seems almost afraid to speak. 'Look at yourself in the mirror,' she urges him. 'You've been wearing the same black clothes for six months now, and they're hanging off you.' — Link to original text

'You mean I'm anorexic, or I just have bad fashion sense? Black is the 'in' colour this year. It's just that you haven't noticed, Mother. You've been too busy since my father's death.' Turning from the full-length mirror, he moves towards her, gripping her hands and pulling her closer. 'Look at yourself for a moment,' he commands. 'My father's been dead for five minutes and you look like you're going to a party.' Hamlet points to the new hot pink dress his mother's wearing. 'It's embarrassing.' — Insight into character

Gertrude sighs. 'Your father died more than six months ago, Hamlet. This is what I mean. You need help. You've changed so much.' — Link to original plot

Hamlet moves to the window. He looks out at the view of the wild Danish sea. His life used to be predictable. Now he feels vulnerable, like the coastline below, buffeted by the waves that crash over it incessantly. — Reflection, figurative language, link to original plot

Just as he is tempted to push the window open and fling himself out, and maybe take his mother with him, there is a knock on the door. A small, dark-haired man is being ushered into the room. 'Ah,' Hamlet says, smiling slightly. 'You must be Dr Fraud, my new shrink.' — Insight into character

'Freud,' his mother corrects him. 'Welcome, Dr Freud. This is my son, Hamlet.' — Lacks conclusion, ends on an uncertain note

1 Definition

Online texts are types of written communication on the world wide web, which form part of the Internet. These texts include a vast amount of information that is accessible through web browsers and can be located using search engines such as Google. The home page is the opening page of a website that introduces the visitor to the purpose and features of the site.

2 Purpose and role of writer

A website exists to provide information or to advertise and to sell products

3 Generic features

Structure and organisation

- written and visual information are designed to attract the eye
- information is arranged in small readable sections
- visual content may dominate
- individual websites vary in text and layout but conform to a general pattern or style

Language

- may be formal or informal according to the subject of the website
- persuasive language
- language specific to the subject of the website may be used
- language to appeal to a certain age, gender or interest group may be used
- language specific to online communities may be used

Grammar

- generally correct language use
- may be impersonal in style; third rather than first person, or inclusive to attract an audience
- imperatives may be used
- sentence fragments may be used

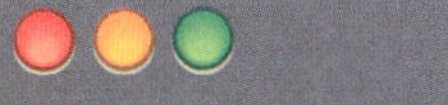

Teen Tours

Website has catchy title

Travel, adventure and much more …

www.teentours.com.au

ABOUT | TRAVEL PROGRAMS | FAQs | CONTACT | BOOKINGS

Home page features

'We travel, not to escape life, but for life not to escape us.'

Use of apt quote

Teen Tours has been taking teenagers to the four corners of the globe for over a decade. We are the experts in travel for young people. You are safe in our hands.

Persuasive language

Persuasive blurb

Browse our travel programs and find a trip to suit your tastes, your wallet and your dreams.

Use of imperatives

Whether your focus is outdoor adventure or cultural and educational pursuits, we have hundreds of affordable, unforgettable adventures with like-minded companions waiting for you.

Appeal to glamour

Emotive language

Check out our photo gallery below. You'll be inspired.

Informality

Photo Gallery

Visual aids

Testimonials:

Fantastic trip to China. Going back next year. So much to see. Alissa, Melbourne, 2018

Rock climbing and rappelling in Costa Rica. Awesome! Don't miss the zip-line through the jungle. Ethan, Mt Gambier, 2018

Cruising the Nile was amazing, but riding a camel around the pyramids at sunrise was the best! Tia and Seth, Perth, 2018

Outside opinions

1 Definition

An informational website offers factual and accurate data to readers on a specific topic.

2 Purpose and role of writer

To present information in a user-friendly and efficient format

3 Generic features

Structure and organisation

- written and visual information are designed to attract the eye
- variation in font size and style to create variety
- information is arranged in small, readable sections
- visual content may dominate
- individual websites vary in text but conform to a general pattern or style

Language

- may be formal or informal according to the subject of the website
- informative language with, maybe, an element of persuasion
- language specific to the content of the website may be used
- language to appeal to a certain age, gender or interest group
- language specific to online communities may be used

Grammar

- generally correct language use
- may use first, second or third person
- imperatives may be used
- sentence fragments may be used

OZZIE TEEN ZINE

ozzieteenscene.com.au

EVENTS GREEN TEEN HEALTH AND WELLBEING CONTACT

Members' Gallery

Zine members rock on at Sydney concert

Happy Zine members on the slopes at Thredbo

Ozzie Teen Zine was created by teens, is written by teens and promotes teenage issues. We pledge to keep you informed of the latest news in music, upcoming events for teens, lifestyle issues and much more. We welcome your input and your feedback.

OZZIE TEEN ZINE

TURNS TWO!

Yes, guys, it's two years since Ozzies Sarah James, Jayshil Singh and Johnno J. Christofis got together and created our Zine.

Happy birthday OTZine!

ZINE MEMBER GRADUATES …

Marcus Ferrero BSc (Hons) – our Green Teen columnist!

FREE! FREE! FREE!

Download

Lean Teen: healthy recipes by Suzy Mee –

*vegetarian

*vegan

*paleo

and more

Member no.

Password

Login

Create an account

Inside:
* Events calendar
* Upcoming concerts
* Surf safari – Byron Bay
* Green news
* Health is wealth …

Features:

- Relevant title
- Attractive home page
- Purpose of website is clear
- Interactive
- Promotional as well as informative
- Images relating to interest group (e.g. teens)
- Inclusive
- Simple instructions
- Positive, enthusiastic tone
- Blend of text and visual images

Glossary

adversarial: an adversary is an enemy. Language that is adversarial creates conflict, an 'us and them' situation

alliteration: the repetition of consonant sounds, especially in poetry

angle: point of view

apt: appropriate

authenticity: genuine, not false or fake

blank verse: verse that doesn't rhyme but has a regular rhythm and metre

byline: the author's name on an article

chronological: according to time sequence, in order

climax: a turning point, the height of a crisis

clincher: a strong concluding sentence or point made in a text

colloquialism: an example of everyday ordinary language

context: the environment in which a text is set

emotional detachment: state of being unemotional, not involved

expletive: swear word

explicit: clear, definite

figurative language: makes comparisons, uses words for dramatic or poetic effect; opposite of literal language

format: layout, procedure

generic: general, rather than specific

genre: a specific text type, e.g. fantasy or crime fiction

hook: a device to gain the reader's interest

hypothesis: a thesis or contention, point of view or angle that is proved in an essay or in writing

imagery: visual language, often figurative language, used in literary texts

imperative: a command or strong advice

inclusive pronoun: such as 'we' and 'our', which includes the reader

irony/ironic: a gap between what is said and what is meant, like sarcasm

literary: writing of a perceived high quality

metaphor: a form of figurative language that compares two objects by saying that one is the other

metaphorical: characteristic or relating to metaphor; figurative

parameter: guideline; the breadth or extent of text

personal referent: reference to the writer to create a closer relationship

personification: to give human qualities to things or animals

primary source: information quoted from an eyewitness

rebuttal: the demolition/rejection of an opponent's argument

reinforce: to strengthen or support

resist: to weaken by disagreement

resolution: the culmination of a plot where conflict is resolved or worked out

rhetorical question: a question that does not require an answer

secondary source: information quoted from a text, as opposed to personal experience or observation

sentence fragment: incomplete sentence, often used to create a dramatic effect

sibilance: the repetition of an 's' sound, particularly in poetry

signpost: indication or hint at the direction a text or story is taking

simile: comparing two objects using the words 'like' or 'as'

speculative fiction: includes science fiction, fantasy, horror or paranormal fiction

subjective: personal as opposed to impersonal; opposite of objective

superlative: adjective denoting the best or the most extreme example of something

terminology: specialist words for a specific subject; also called metalanguage

testimonial: endorsement by experts

uncluttered: spare in detail, not overdone

Writing activities

1. **Advertisement:** Develop your own advertisement for a product aimed at teenagers.
2. **Agenda and minutes:** Write up the minutes of an imaginary sporting club meeting.
3. **Biography:** Research the life of a famous person who interests you, and write a chapter detailing an important part of his or her life.
4. **Blog:** Write an entertaining blog on a subject that interests you.
5. **Brochure/flyer:** Create either of these items to market a new product.
6. **Description:** Practise writing an informative and a literary description about your favourite place, to develop both writing styles.
7. **Editorial:** Write an editorial on a controversial issue. Read a newspaper to find a topic.
8. **Essay: comparative:** Discuss, or compare the issues revealed in, a feature film and a work of prose fiction.
9. **Essay: persuasive:** Write a persuasive essay on an issue you feel strongly about.
10. **Feature article:** As a journalist, write a feature article on a newsworthy item, bringing more depth and background to the subject.
11. **Job application: letter and resume:** Write a job application in an area of the work force that interests you. Add a resume.
12. **Job interview:** Now write an imaginary interview in which you demonstrate your aptitude for the job above.
13. **Letter: business:** Write a business letter of complaint about a faulty product.
14. **Letter to the editor:** Write a persuasive letter to the editor on an issue you feel strongly about.
15. **Narrative genres:** Choose one of the narrative genres modelled earlier in the book and write a story conforming to the guidelines for that genre.
16. **News article:** Write a news article on a topic that interests you: real or imaginary.
17. **Nonfiction:** Comment on the ways in which nonfiction can introduce us to new ideas and experiences.
18. **Novel essay:** Write an analytical essay on a novel that you have read recently. Analyse the perspectives and representations revealed in a novel you are studying in class.
19. **Play essay:** How entertaining is a modern play you have seen, read or studied in class? Does it persuade you to a particular point of view?
20. **Poetry analysis:** Choose a poem you particularly like, or your own poem, and write a short analysis of it.

21 **Report:** Isolate a problem in your community or in society. Do some research and present your findings in report format.

22 **Research assignment and reference list:** Choose a historical era or an environmental topic that interests you, develop a hypothesis and write up a referenced assignment with a correctly set out reference list.

23 **Review: documentary:** View and review a documentary, evaluating its effectiveness as a nonfiction film.

24 **Review: film:** Review a film that you have seen lately either at the cinema, on TV, DVD or streamed.

25 **Review: play:** Read or view a play and write a review of it for a newspaper.

26 **Shakespearean drama:** Find a famous speech from a Shakespearean play and analyse its meaning and its blank verse.

27 **Shakespearean essay:** Write an analytical essay on an aspect of the Shakespearean play that you are studying.

28 **Short story:** Write a short story with a twist.

29 **Song:** Compose your own song.

30 **Speech: monologue:** Select a character from a text you have studied this year, and write a monologue that reflects their thoughts or attitudes towards issues in the text.

31 **Speech: occasional:** Write a speech to be delivered on an important social occasion.

32 **Speech: text-based:** Use a literary text as the basis of a speech on a special subject or issue. Consider adding multimodal features to your presentation.

33 **Textual intervention:** Write a prelude, interlude or postlude chapter to add to the novel that you are studying.

34 **Textual reconstruction:** Select a minor character in a text you have studied and reconstruct a key scene from their point of view.

35 **Website: corporate:** Create an informative and persuasive corporate website for teenagers.

36 **Website: informational:** Create an informational website for community use.

Table of text types

Creative

- Biography
- Description: literary
- Narrative genre:
  - teenage romance
  - speculative fiction
- Play script: writing and performing
- Short story
- Song
- Speech: monologue
- Textual intervention
- Textual reconstruction

Informative

- Agenda and minutes
- Biography
- Blog
- Description: informative
- Essay:
  - comparative
  - persuasive
- Feature article
- Job application:
  - letter
  - resume
- Job interview
- Letter: business
- News article
- Nonfiction
- Novel: essay
- Play: modern drama essay
- Poetry: analysis
- Report
- Research assignment
- Review:
  - documentary
  - film
  - play
- Shakespearean drama: aspects and analysis
- Shakespearean drama: essay
- Speech:
  - occasional
  - text-based
- Website:
  - corporate
  - informational

Literary

- Description: literary
- Essay: comparative
- Nonfiction
- Novel: essay
- Poetry: analysis
- Play:
  - modern drama essay
  - script
  - Shakespearean drama
- Short story
- Speech: monologue
- Textual intervention
- Textual reconstruction

Media

- Advertisement
- Blog
- Brochure/flyer
- Editorial
- Feature article
- Letter to the editor
- News article
- Review:
  - documentary
  - film
  - play
- Website:
  - corporate
  - informational

Persuasive

- Advertisement
- Blog
- Brochure/flyer
- Editorial
- Essay: persuasive
- Job application: letter
- Job interview
- Letter to the editor
- Research assignment
- Review:
  - documentary
  - film
  - play
- Speech: occasional
- Website:
  - corporate
  - informational

Spoken

- Job interview
- Play script: writing and performing
- Speech:
  - monologue
  - occasional
  - text-based